About

I am a multimedia artist who hails from the UK. I work in drawing, video animation and film making, with parallels between contemporary work and the theories and practices of Constructivism, Surrealism, Expressionism and Futurism.

My degree was in Fine Art (Digital New Media, Contemporary Art History, Curatorship) at Lancaster University, First-Class Honours. Since graduating in July 2012 my work has been exhibited in selected group and solo shows and published in national and international art magazines and websites, including the Aesthetica Art Prize 2012, and the 100 Contemporary Artists 2013 Anthology, Jerwood Drawing Prize 2013 and screening at the 20th IDFF Off Cinema Film Festival, Poznan and the Grand Off World Independent Film Awards, Warsaw, Poland.

I am now pursuing a long-term journey of a flaneur documenting architecture in the former Eastern Bloc – the group of socialist states of Central and Eastern Europe. To date I have visited the following countries: Belarus, Bulgaria, Czech Republic, Germany, Hungary, Latvia, Lithuania, Poland, Slovakia and Ukraine. I am seldom interested in the ideology or social concepts that often associates these buildings with a totalitarian regime. Instead, creating a multimedia archive of the buildings, which currently have little or no documentation, are set to be demolished or remain abandoned. As part of my ongoing exploration I often stay with locals in residential areas of cities as a means to understand the communities that surround the architecture and the nature of decay. I hope to highlight the importance of protecting structures, such as communal living, recreation, aviation, industrialisation, urban planning and communication.

This book brings together my exploration in the former Eastern Bloc and ultimately has brought me to Russia in 2021 where my cultural and architectural fascination and adventure continues.

© JORDAN L RODGERS 2021 ALL RIGHTS RESERVED, DO NOT USE.

Обо мне

Я мультимедийный художник из Великобритании. Я работаю в сфере искусства, видео, анимации и создания фильмов и провожу параллели между современной работой и теориями и практиками конструктивизма, сюрреализма, экспрессионизма и футуризма.

Я получил диплом с отличием в области изобразительного искусства (новые цифровые средства массовой информации, история современного искусства, кураторство) в Ланкастерском университете. После выпуска в июле 2012 года мои работы были выставлены на групповых и персональных экспозициях и опубликованы в национальных и международных художественных журналах и на веб-сайтах, в том числе таких, как: Aesthetica Art Prize 2012, 100 Contemporary Artists 2013 Anthology, Jerwood Drawing Prize 2013, 20-ый фестиваль фильмов IDFF Off Cinema Познань и Grand Off World Independent Film Awards Варшава, Польша.

Сейчас я продолжаю свое путешествие фланера, документирующего архитектуру бывшего Восточного блока – группы социалистических государств Центральной и Восточной Европы. На сегодняшний день я побывал в следующих странах: Республика Беларусь, Болгария, Чехия, Германия, Венгрия, Латвия, Литва, Польша, Словакия и Украина. Мой интерес редко вызывают идеология или же социальные концепции, которые существовали во времена постройки данной архитектуры и которые связывают данные строения с тоталитарным режимом. Вместо этого я создаю мультимедийный архив зданий, которые в настоящее время практически не имеют документации, подлежат сносу или же являются заброшенными. В рамках моих постоянных исследований я часто взаимодействую с местными жителями, проживающих в данных городах, чтобы понять сообщества, которые окружают архитектуру и природу распада. Я надеюсь, подчеркнуть важность защиты структур таких, как общественная жизнь, отдых, авиация, индустриализация, городское планирования и коммуникации.

Данная книга, объединившая все мои исследования, касающиеся бывшего Восточного блока, в конечном итоге привела меня в Россию в 2021 году, где мои культурные и архитектурные приключения продолжаются.

© ДЖОРДАН Л. РОДЖЕРС 2021 ВСЕ ПРАВА ЗАЩИЩЕНЫ, НЕ ИСПОЛЬЗОВАТЬ.

SELECTED SOLO EXHIBITION
2021, Drawing Russia 2021, Moscow, Russia
2020, Śląsk węglem szkicowany, Szyb Maciej, Zabrze, Poland
2019, Drawing: Katowice, International Congress Center (MCK), Katowice, Poland
2017, iPad Drawing: Architektura Bloku Wschodniego, Fundacja New Era Art Gallery, Krakow, Poland
2014, Drawing: Liverpool, Clove Hitch Gallery, Liverpool
2013, New Babylon, Nancy Victor Gallery, London

SELECTED GROUP EXHIBITION
2017, GEOFILMFESTIVAL and EXPOCINEMA, Padova, Italy
2016, Grand Off World Independent Film Awards, Warsaw, Poland
2016, IndieWise Virtual Festival, Miami, Florida
2016, Second Asia International (Wenzhou) Youth Micro-Film Exhibition, Ministry of Culture of The People's Republic of China
2016, Festiwal Popularyzatorów Filmowych Bytom Film Festiwal, Poland
2016, In/Out Video & Film Festival: Ethics Attention & Intention, Moore College of Art, Philadelphia, Pennsylvania
2016, Take a look into Nowa Huta (Zajrzyj do Huty), ARTzona Museum of History of Nowa Huta, Krakow, Poland
2016, 20th IDFF Off Cinema Film Festival, Poznań, Poland
2016, Ekofilm Festival, Nowogard, Poland
2016, Wildlife Vaasa Festival-International Nature Film Festival, Vaasa, Finland
2016, The Quarantine Film Festival, Varna, Bulgaria
2016, TimeLine Film Festival 2016, Italy
2016, Goldensun Short Film Festival, Malta
2016, EsX Film Festival, Novi Sad, Serbia
2016, Pocket Cinema Film Festival, Pakistan American Cultural Centre, Asia
2016, Emerge Film Festival, Auburn, ME
2015, International Green Culture Festival, Belgrade, Serbia
2015, Environment Art Speaks Out, Istanbul Modern Museum, Turkey, Istanbul
2015, Visionaria22 International Film Festival 2015, Italy, Siena
2015, Innsbruck Nature Film Festival 2015, Austria
2015, Bogotá Experimental Film Festival / CineAutopsia, Spain
2015, Handle Climate Change Film Festival 2015, Shenzhen, China
2015, Tassie eco Film Fest, Hobart, Tasmania
2015, Frame By Sound, Apple Store Soho, New York, NY
2015, Electric Open Art 2015, Electric Picture House, Cheshire
2015, Disaster Is My Muse, Venice Arts Gallery, Los Angeles
2015, Athens Animation Festival 2015, Athens
2015, ProxyACT International Short Film Festival, London
2015, Festival Parachute Light Zero Act II, Paris
2014, 6th Cairo Video Festival 2014, Medrar, Cairo
2014, How Many?, PatchWork, Local Creation, Altrincham
2014, Home, Bridewell Studios & Gallery, Liverpool
2014, Exploring Boundaries, neo:gallery 22, Bolton
2014, Live.Art.Liverpool, MetQuarter, Liverpool
2014, Encounters Journeys & Discoveries, BAR Gallery, London
2014, Digital, Unframed, LLC, New Mexico

2013, University of Liverpool, Histories Languages and Cultures Gallery academic year 2013/14
2013, Bees Make Honey Creative Community, Memories of the Future in Pictures, Nottingham
2013, Jerwood Drawing Prize 2013, Jerwood Space, London
2013, Canned International Film Festival, Cheshire
2013, Place/Non-Place: Locality in the Digital Age, Venice Arts Gallery, Los Angeles
2013, Possible Impossibilities, Liverpool Art Month, Bridewell Studios & Gallery, Liverpool
2013, Fresh Meat Gallery Open 2013 in collaboration with Cornflake, London
2013, Aesthetica Art Prize Exhibition 2013, York St Marys, York
2013, Art In Mind Downtown, The Brick Lane Gallery, London
2013, Affordable Art Exhibition Vol.6, Vibe Gallery, London
2013, Open Call Exhibition, Madelainartz Gallery, Liverpool
2012, Maidstone Film Festival, Stepping Stone Studios, Kent
2012, Open Call Exhibition, Fallout Factory 97, Liverpool
2012, Lancaster University Fine Art Degree Show, We Were Here, Peter Scott Gallery, Lancaster

EDUCATION
2009 - 2012, BA Hons Fine Art (Digital New Media, Contemporary Art History, Curatorship), Lancaster University, First-Class

INTERNSHIP
2014, Digital Artist/ Animator, Hope Street Ltd Emerging Artist Programme 2014

PRIZES
2015, Short-list, Innsbruck Nature Film Festival 2015
2013, Short-list, Jerwood Drawing Prize 2013
2012, Long-list, Aesthetica Art Prize 2012, and the 100 Contemporary Artists 2013 Anthology

TV WORK DOCUMENTARY
TVP info, Poland and Lithuania
Śląska tea o'clock, 13.09.2020

THEATRE
2014, Control 25, FACT, Liverpool
2014, This Must Be The Place, Constellations, Liverpool
2014, Race Against Time, thebluecoat, Liverpool
2014, Spring Heeled Jack, Everton Park, Everton
2014, Sense and Sustainability, thebluecoat, Liverpool

iPAD DRAWING WORKSHOPS
2014, iPad Art Class: Cityscapes at Apple Store, Covent Garden, London
2013, Jerwood Drawing Prize: The Big Draw, London
2013, Making Tracks Workshop Performance, Rich Mix Shoreditch, London
2013, Tea With An Architect: Love Architecture Festival, Liverpool

CHARITY WORK
Crohn's and Colitis UK, Davis Family YMCA for arts & humanities, Kidney Research UK, Macmillan Cancer Care, the Prince's Trust, the Trafford and South Manchester - Mobile Artistic Mental Health and Wellbeing Service

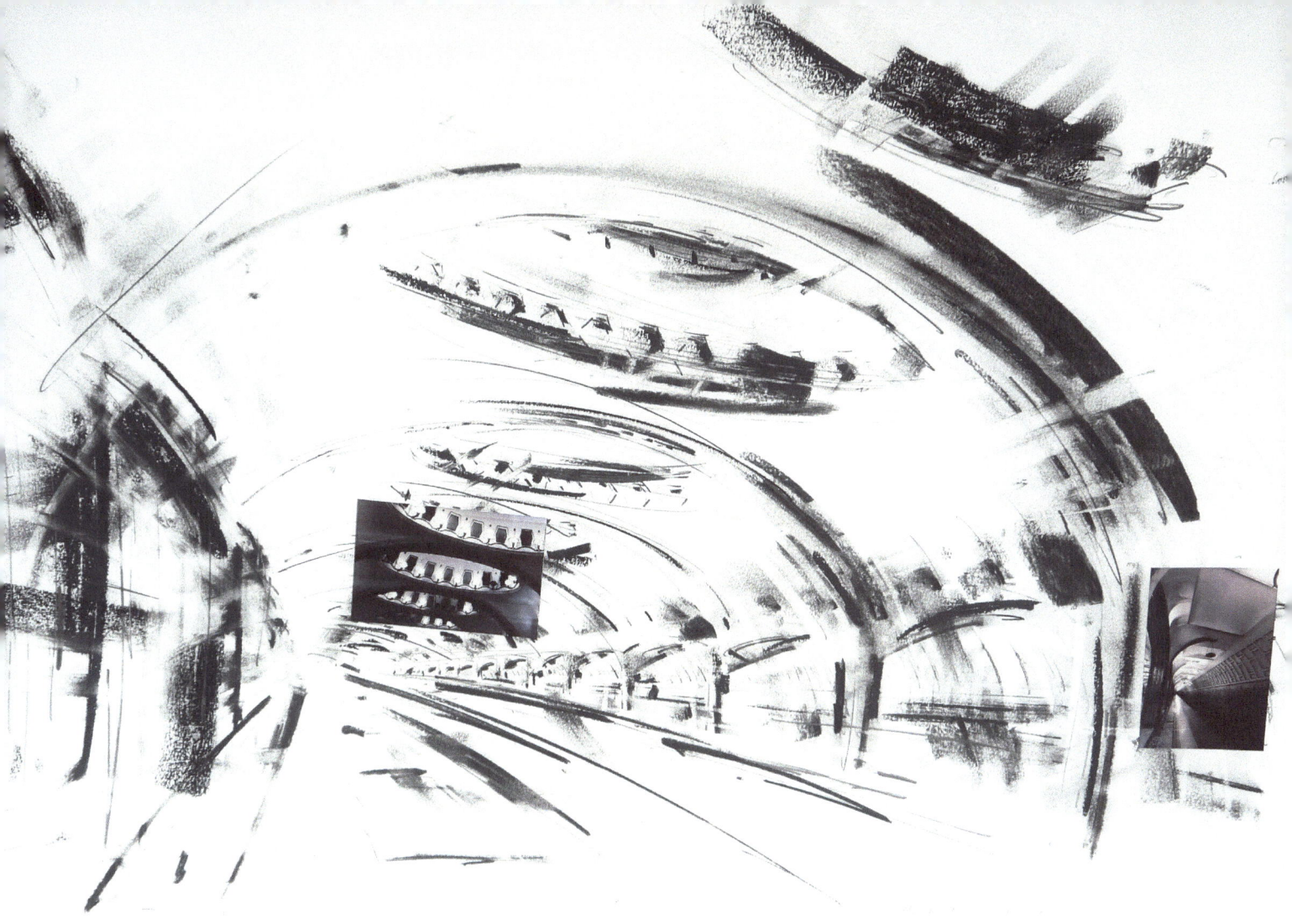

Mayakovskaya

Маяковская

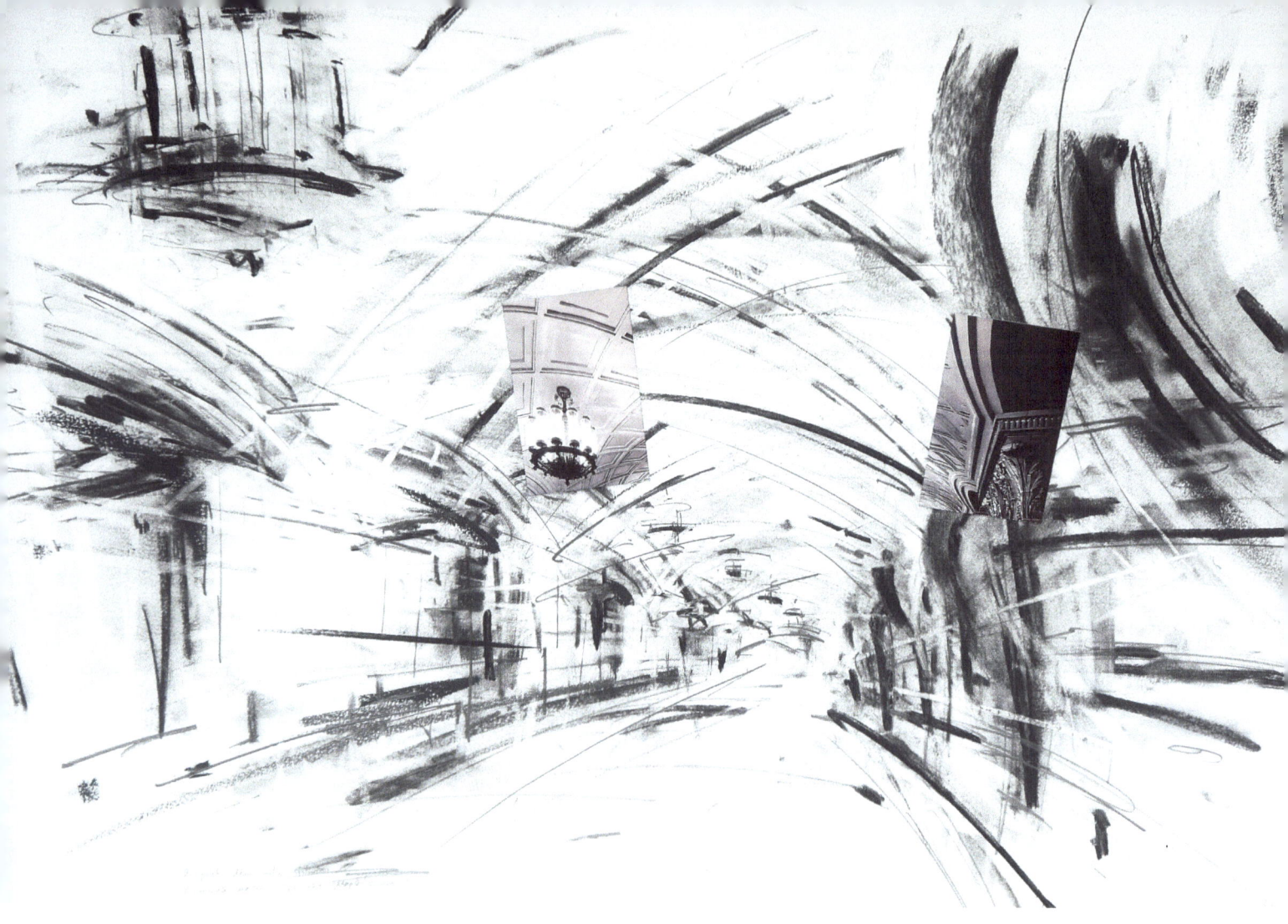

Prospekt Mira

Проспе́кт Ми́ра

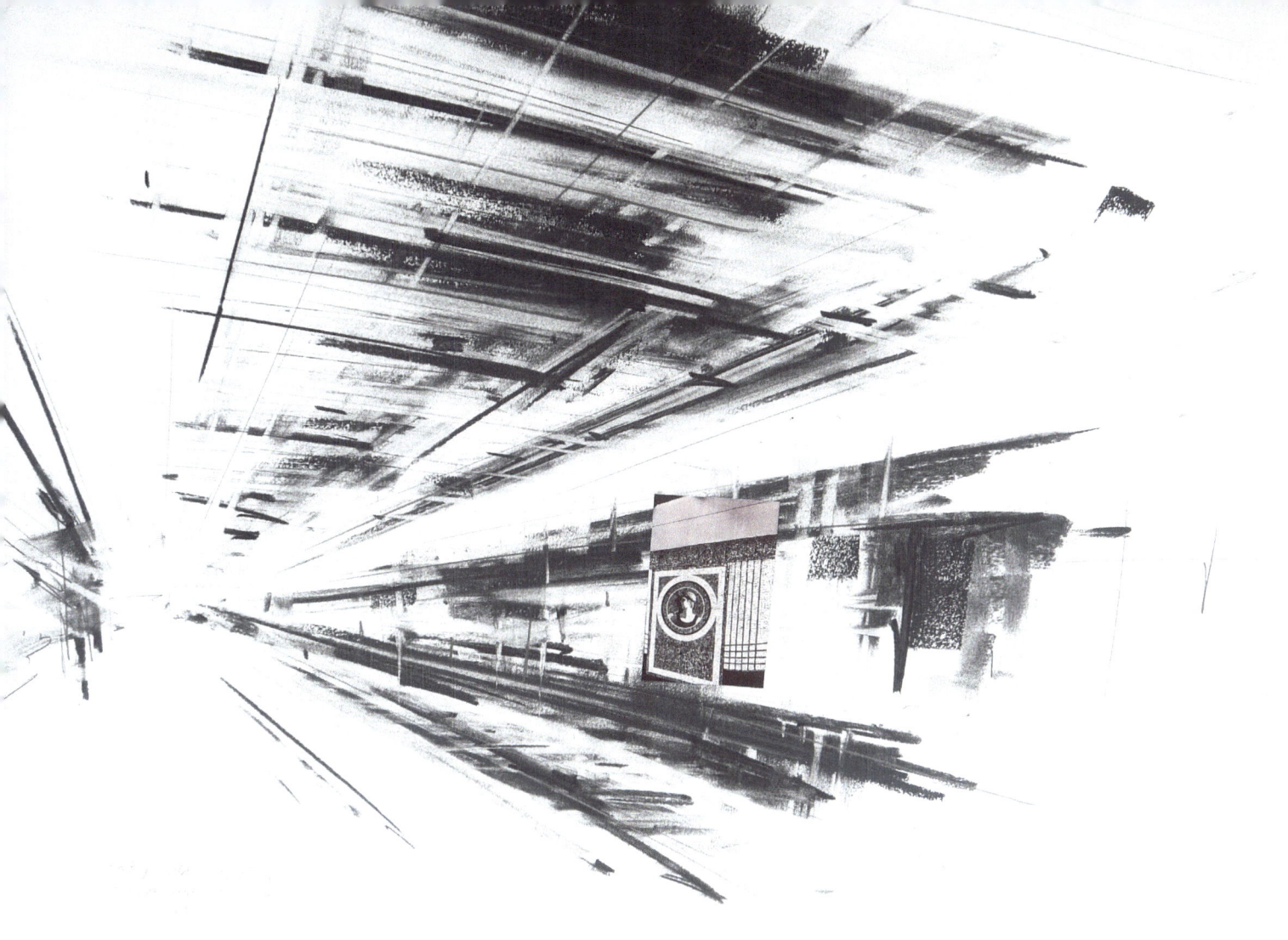

Sportivnaya

ст. м. Спортивная

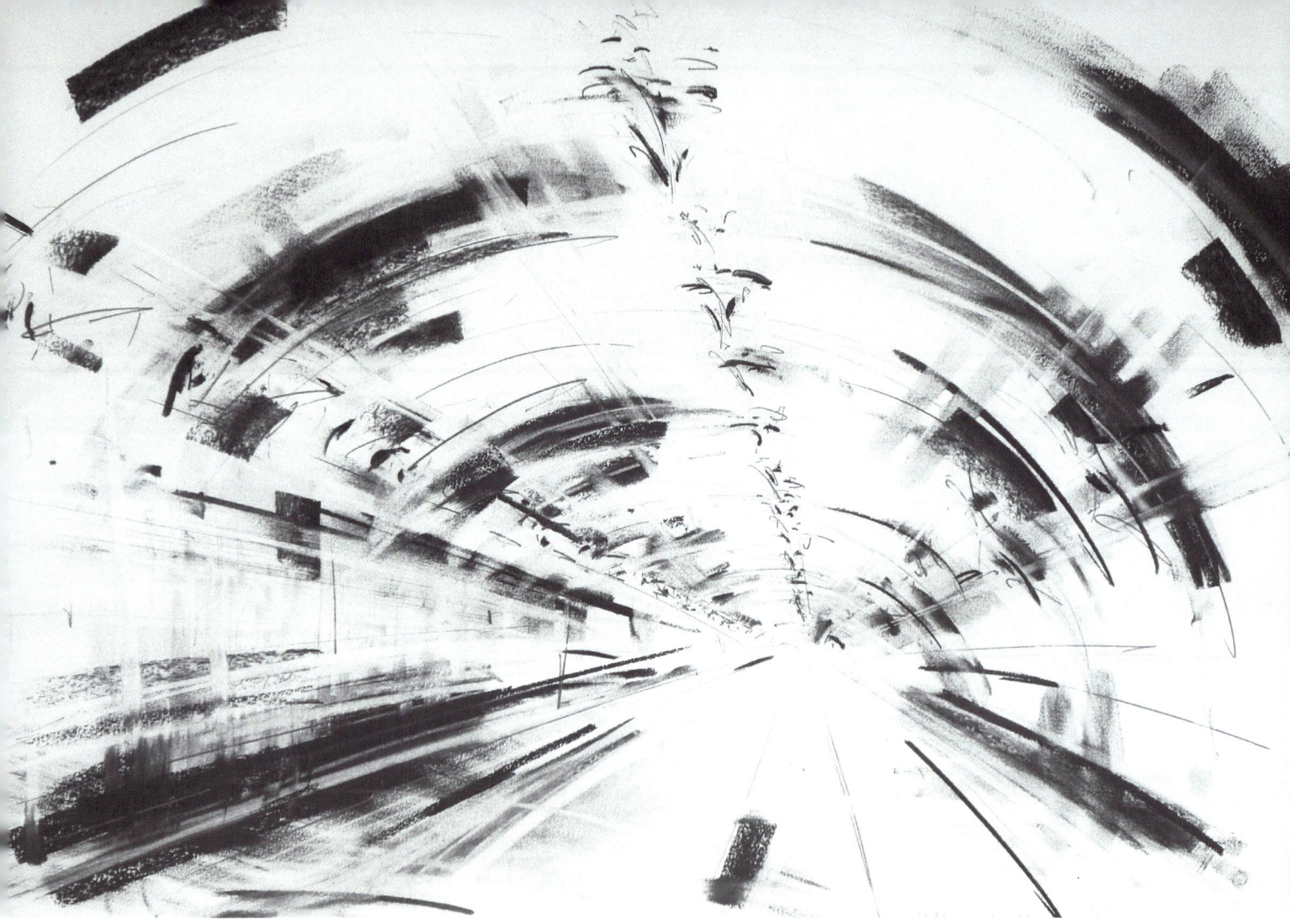

Arbatskaya

8

Арба́тская

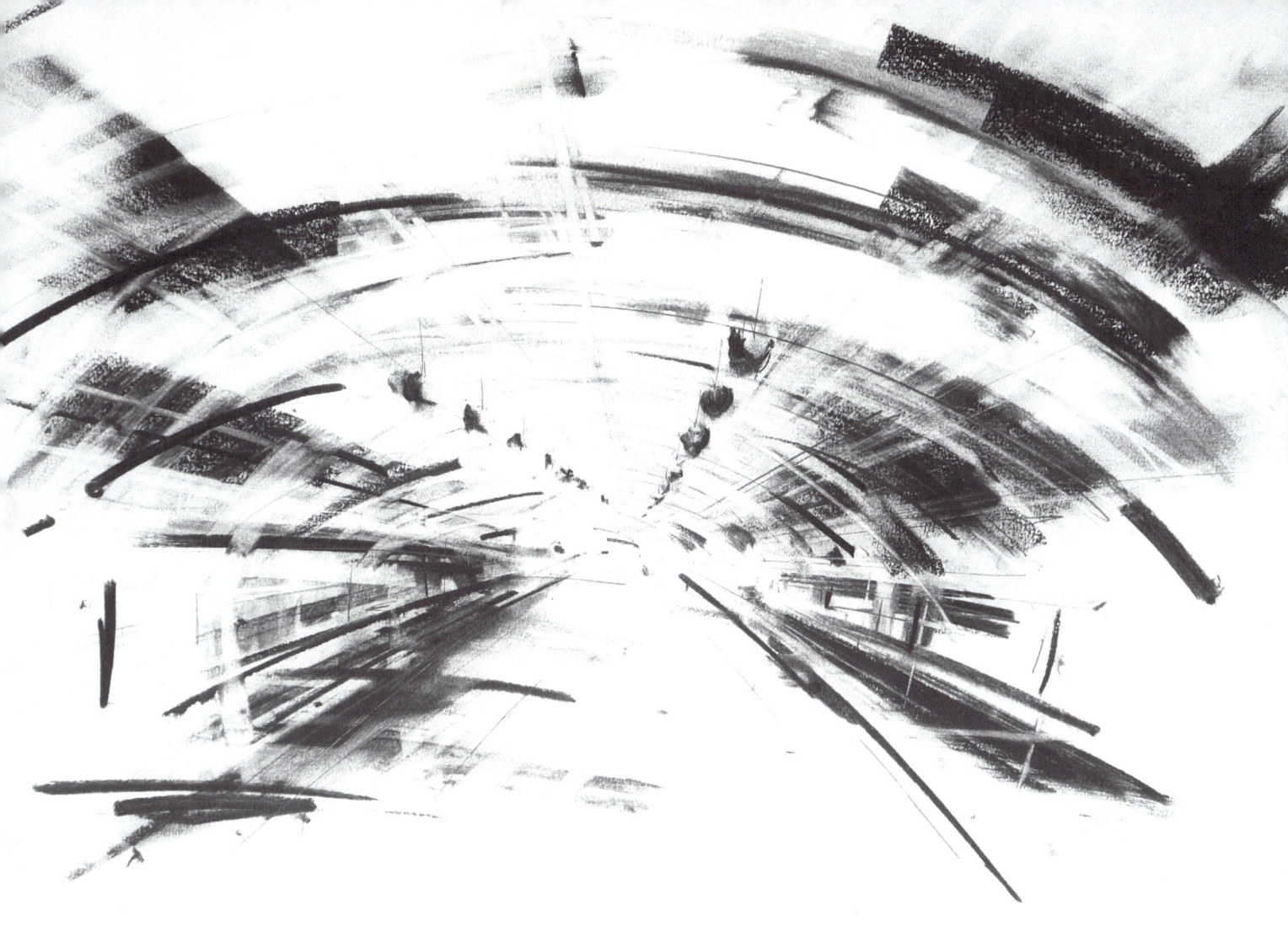

Biblioteka imeni Lenina

Библиоте́ка и́мени Ле́нина

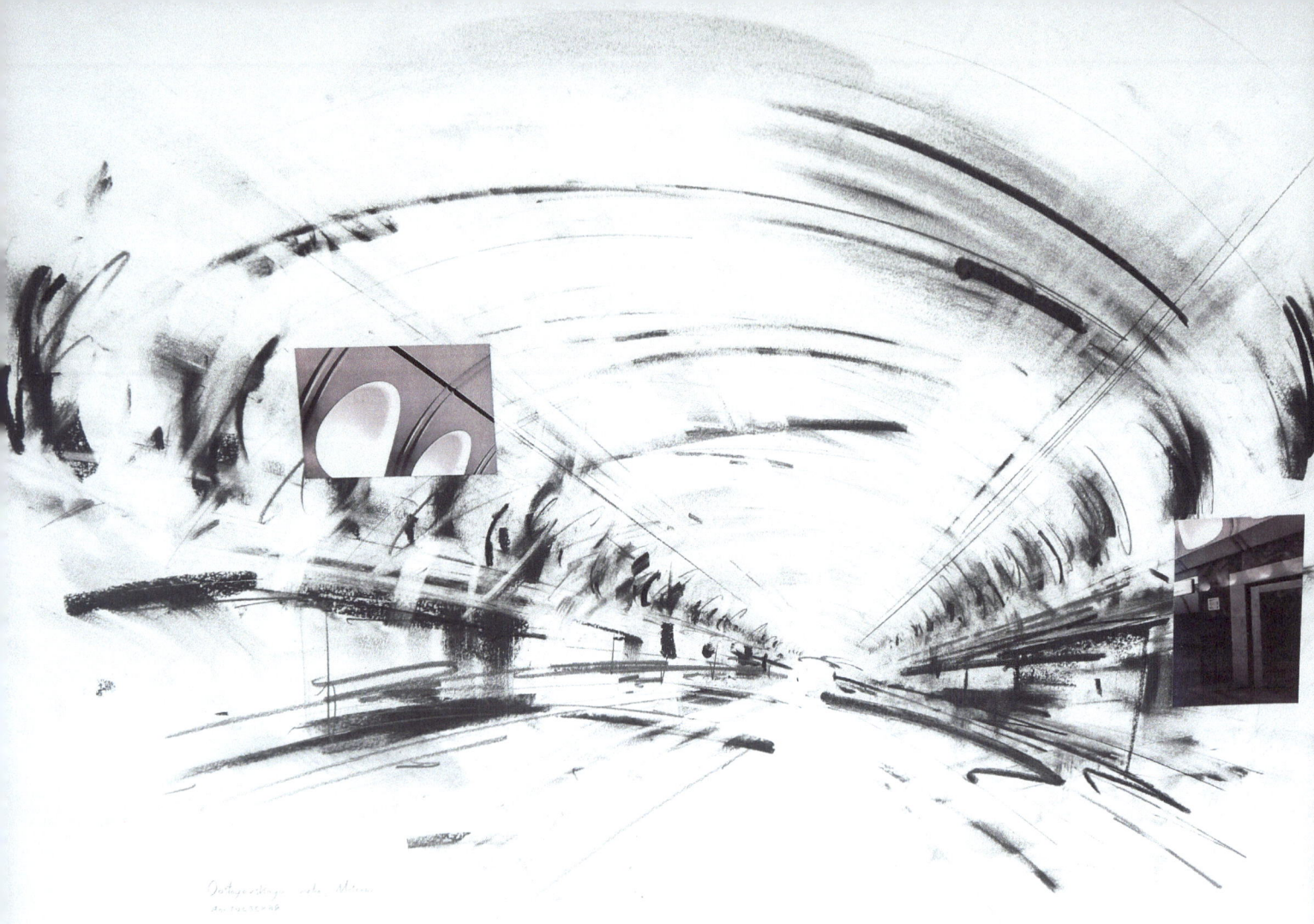

Dostoyevskaya metro

Достоевская

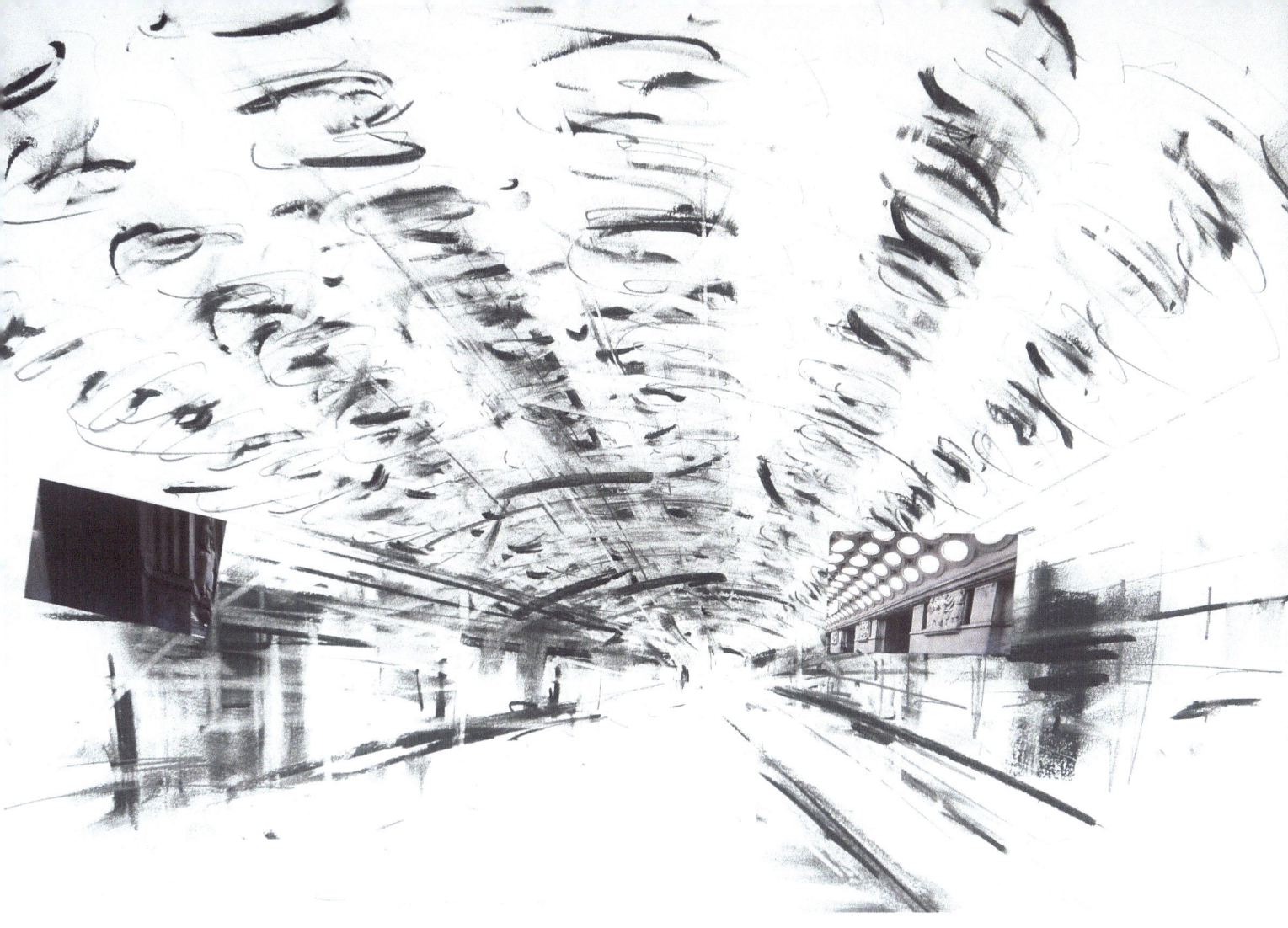

Elektrozavodskaya

11

Электрозаво́дская

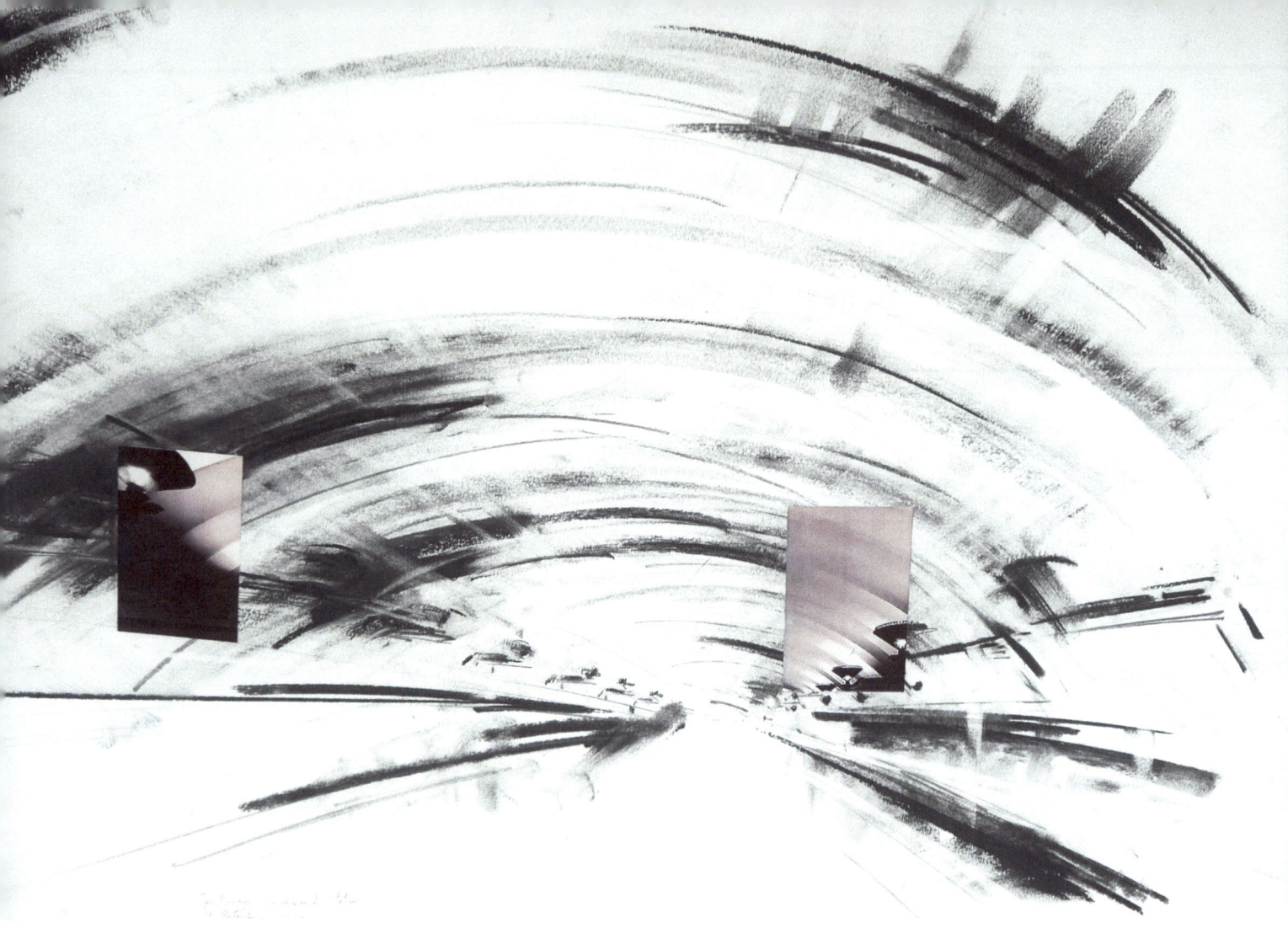

Sportivnaya station

ст. м. Спортивная

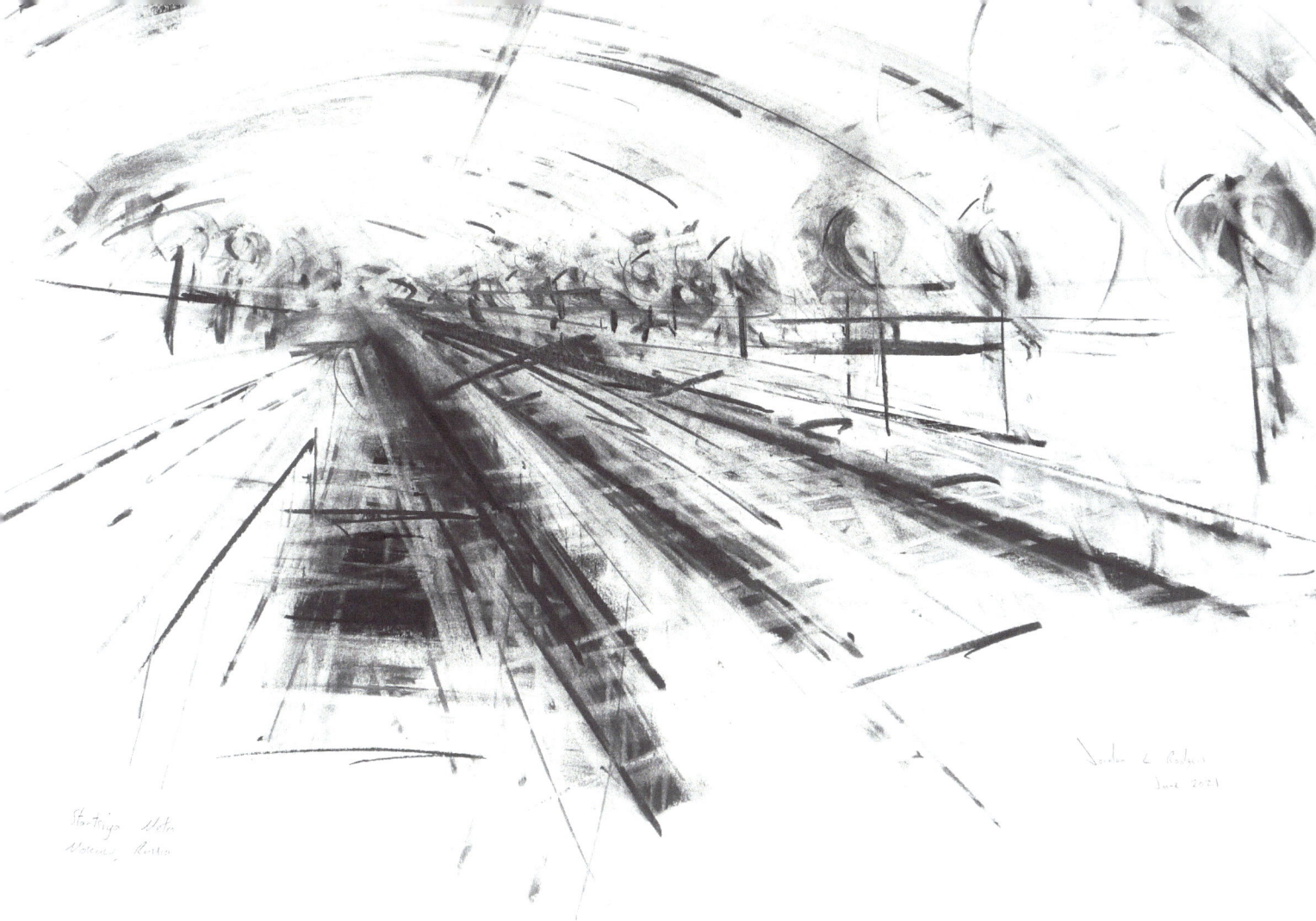

Park Kultury

Парк культуры

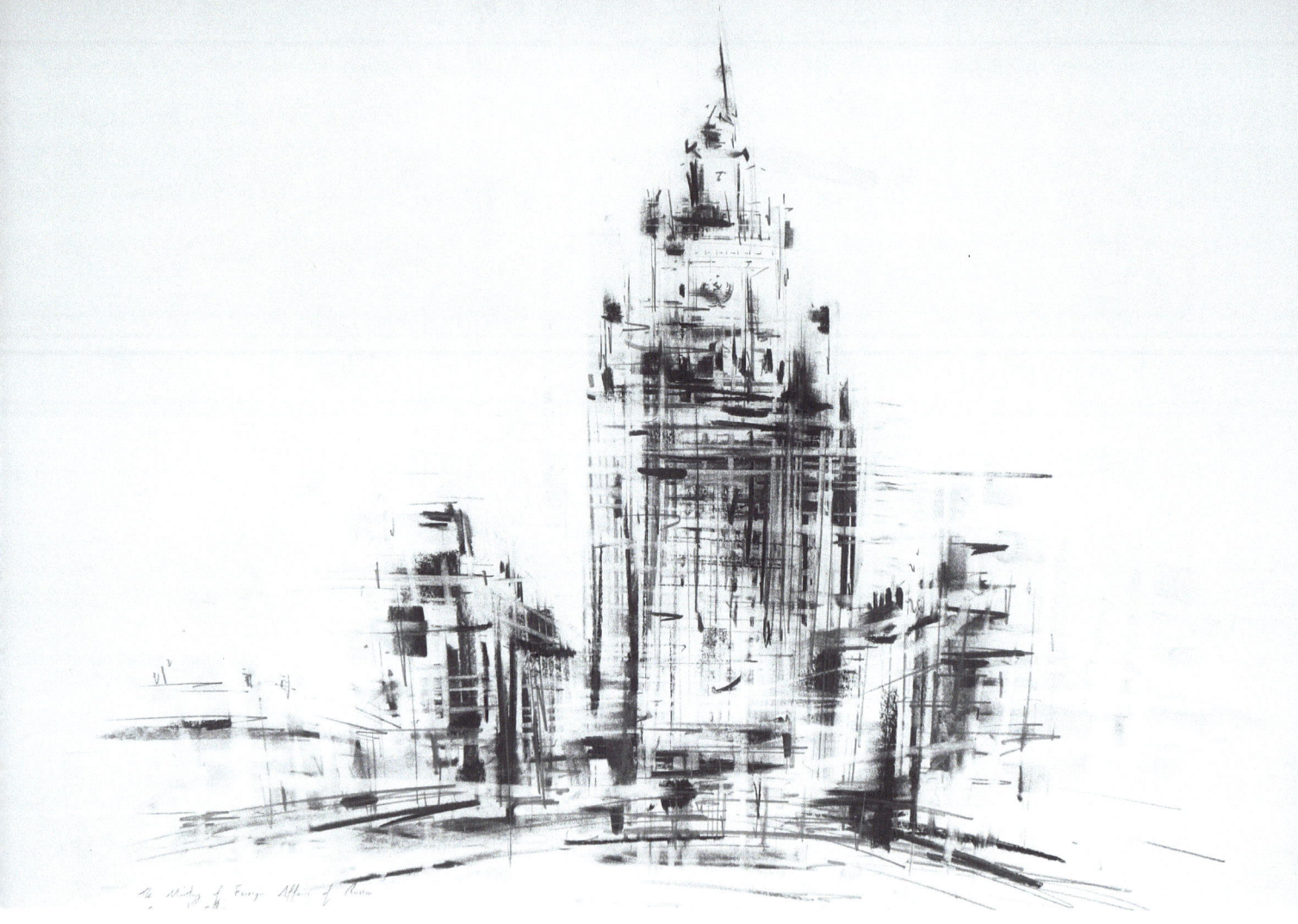

The Ministry of Foreign Affairs of Russia

Министерство иностранных дел России

The Hilton Moscow Leningradskaya

Хилтон Москоу Ленинградская

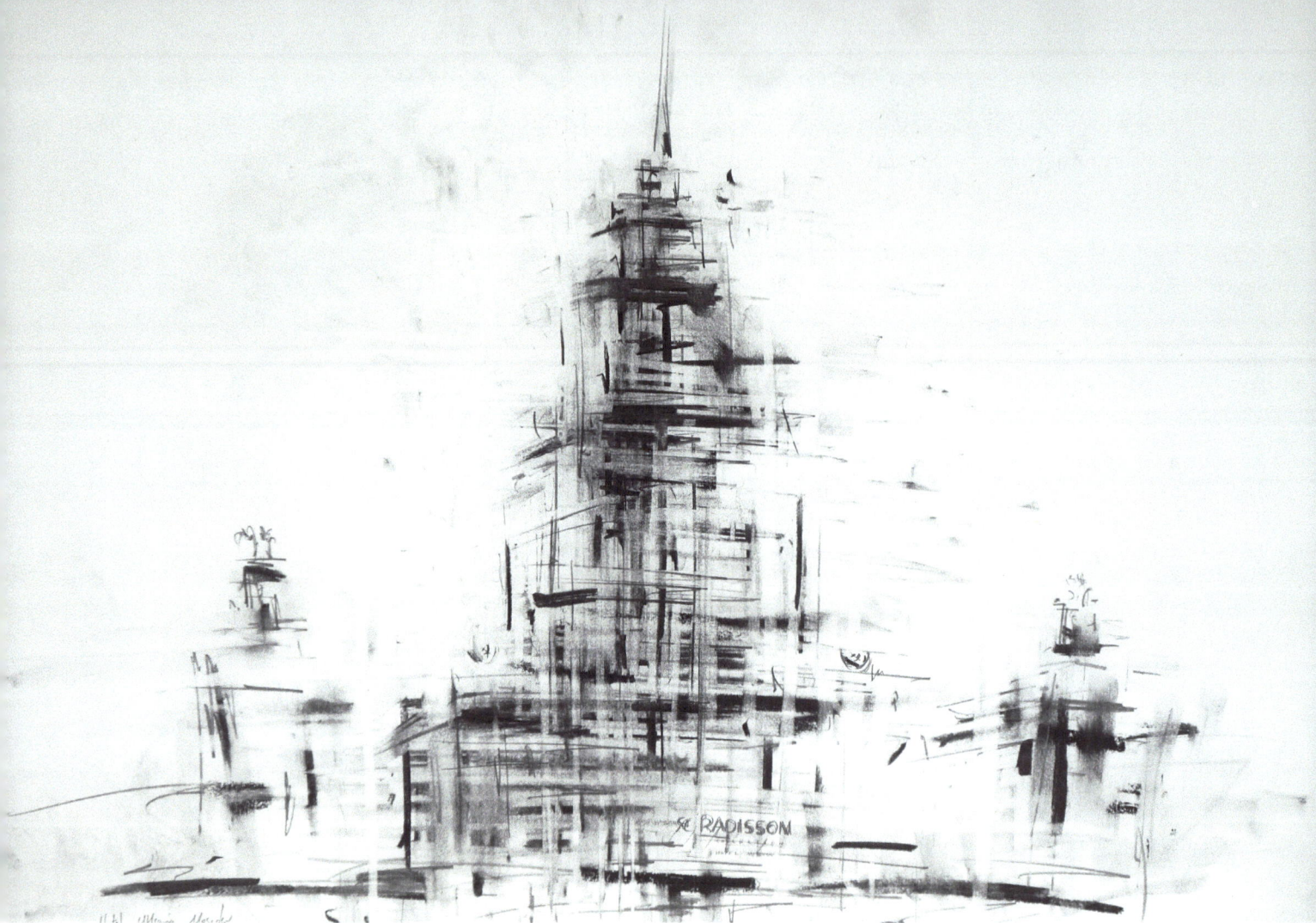

Hotel Ukraina

Гостиница Украина

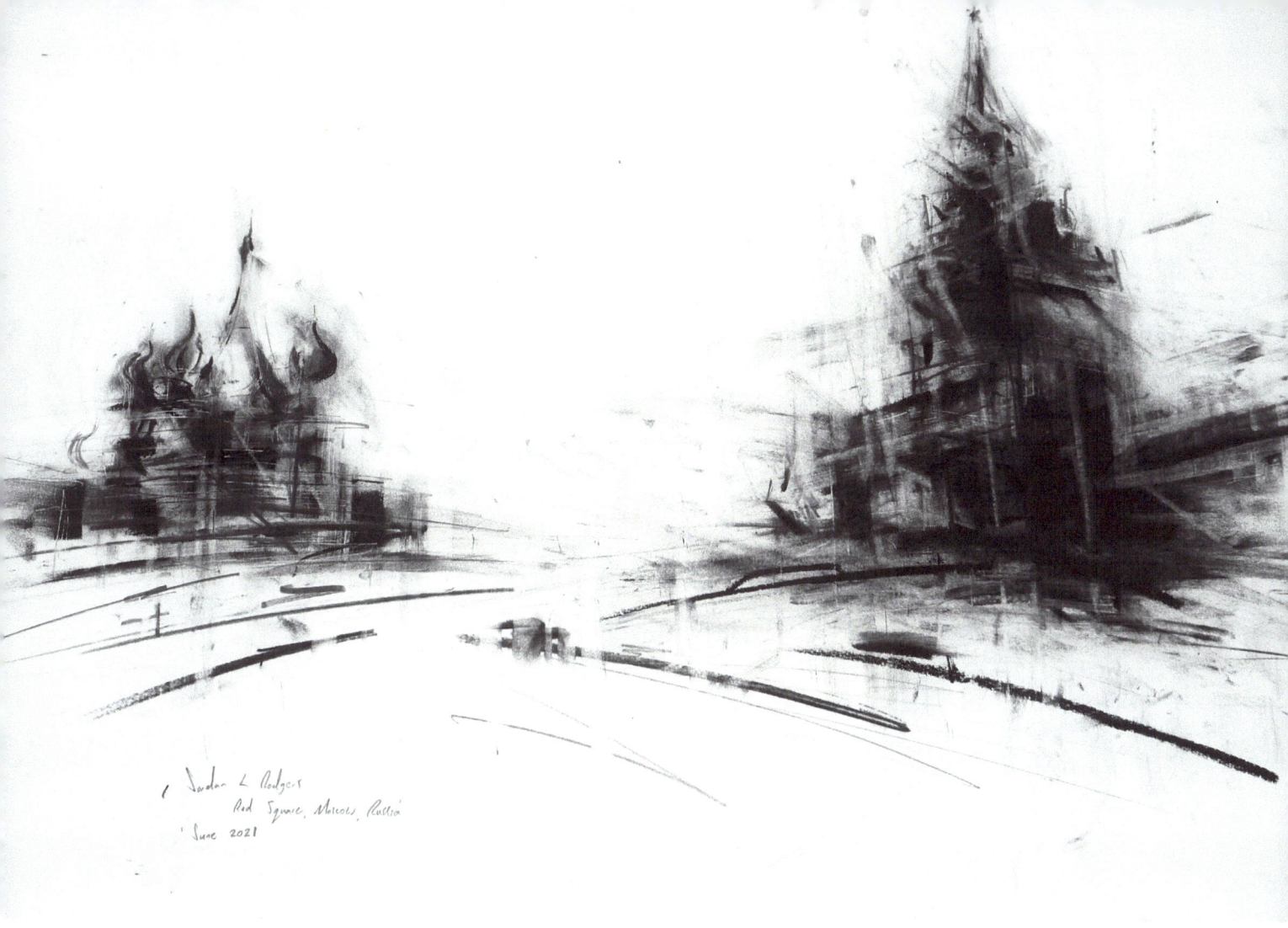

Red Square

17

Krasnaya ploshchad'

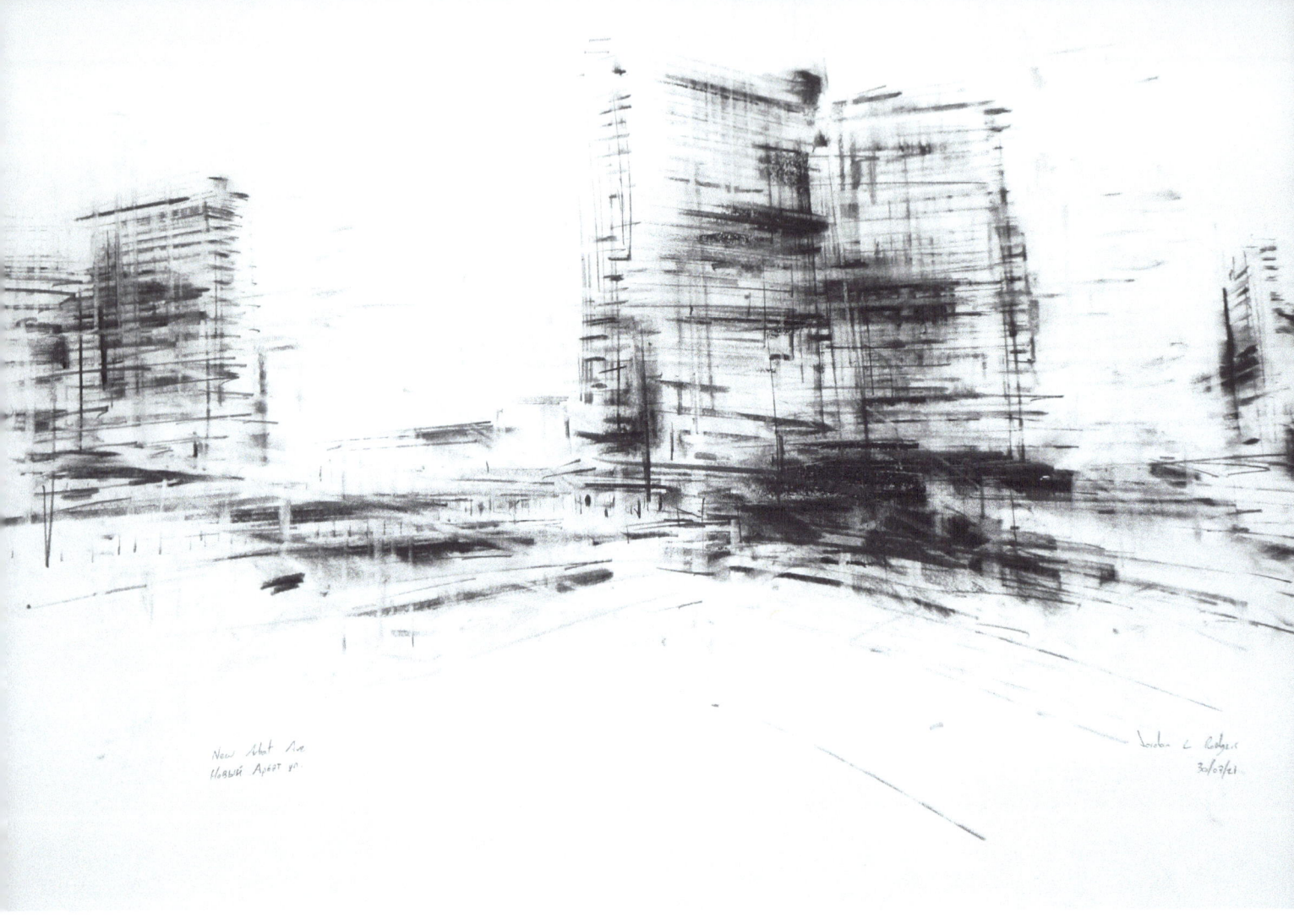

New Arbat Avenue

Но́вый Арба́т

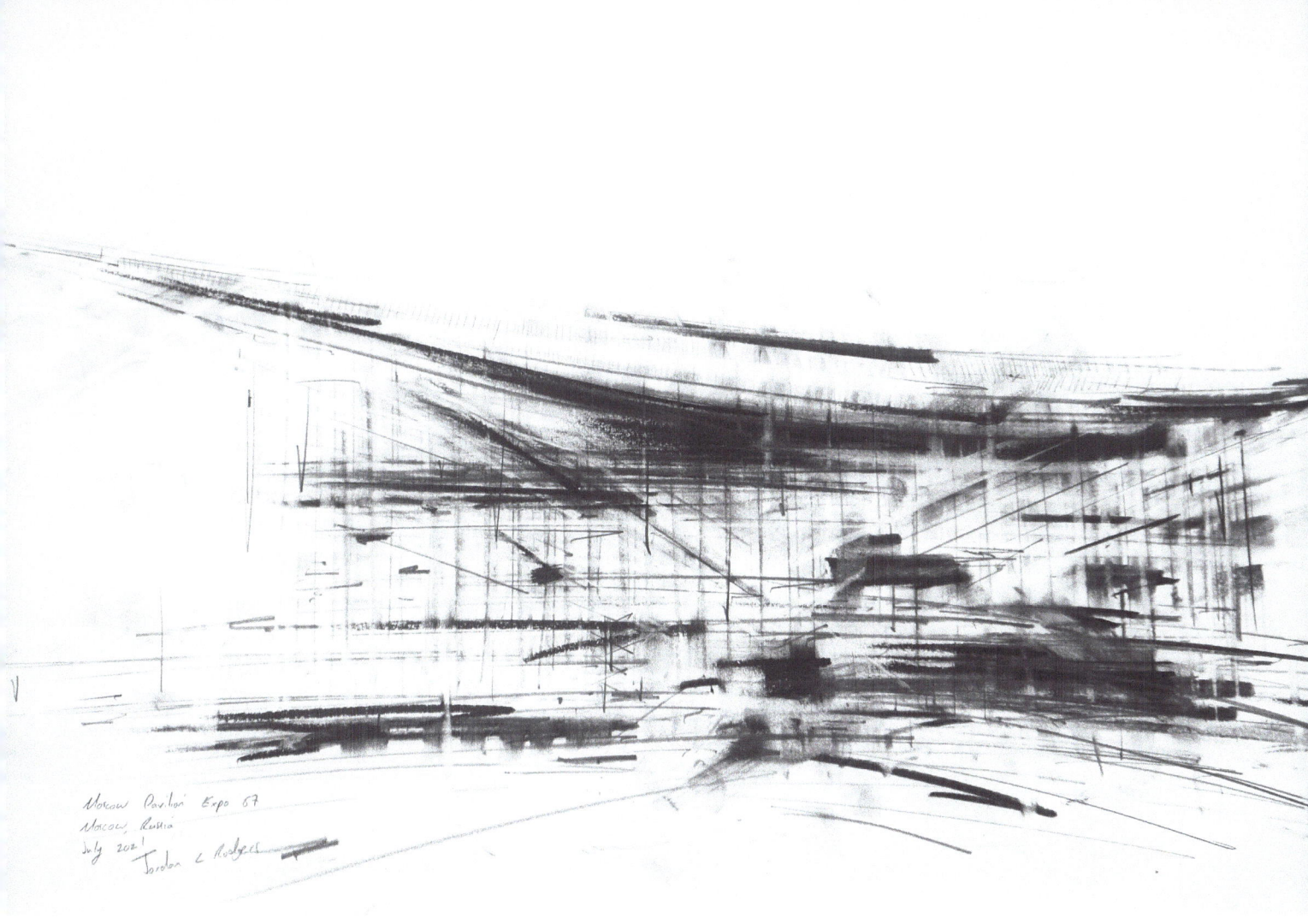

The Moscow Pavilion (former expo67 Pavilion)

19

Павильон № 70 Москва

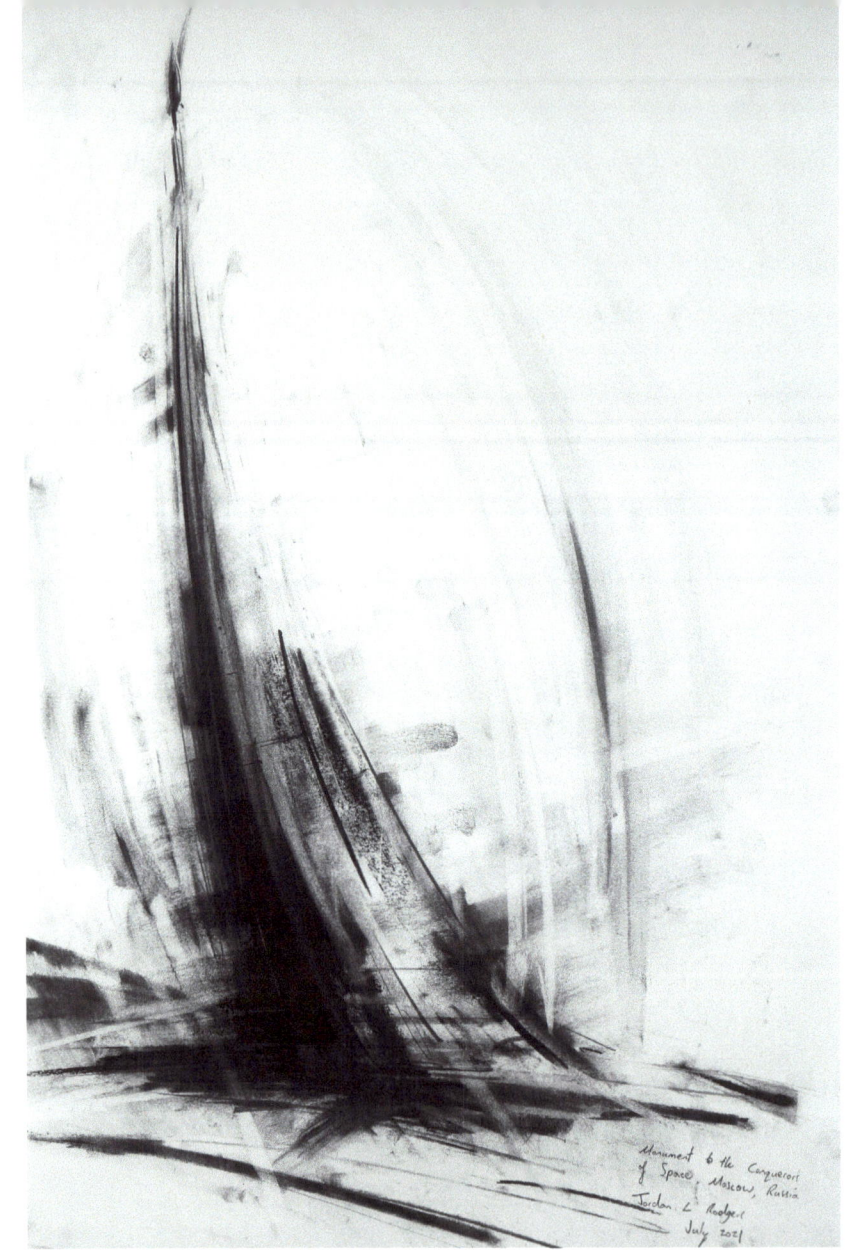

Space Conquerors Monument

Монумент покорителям космоса

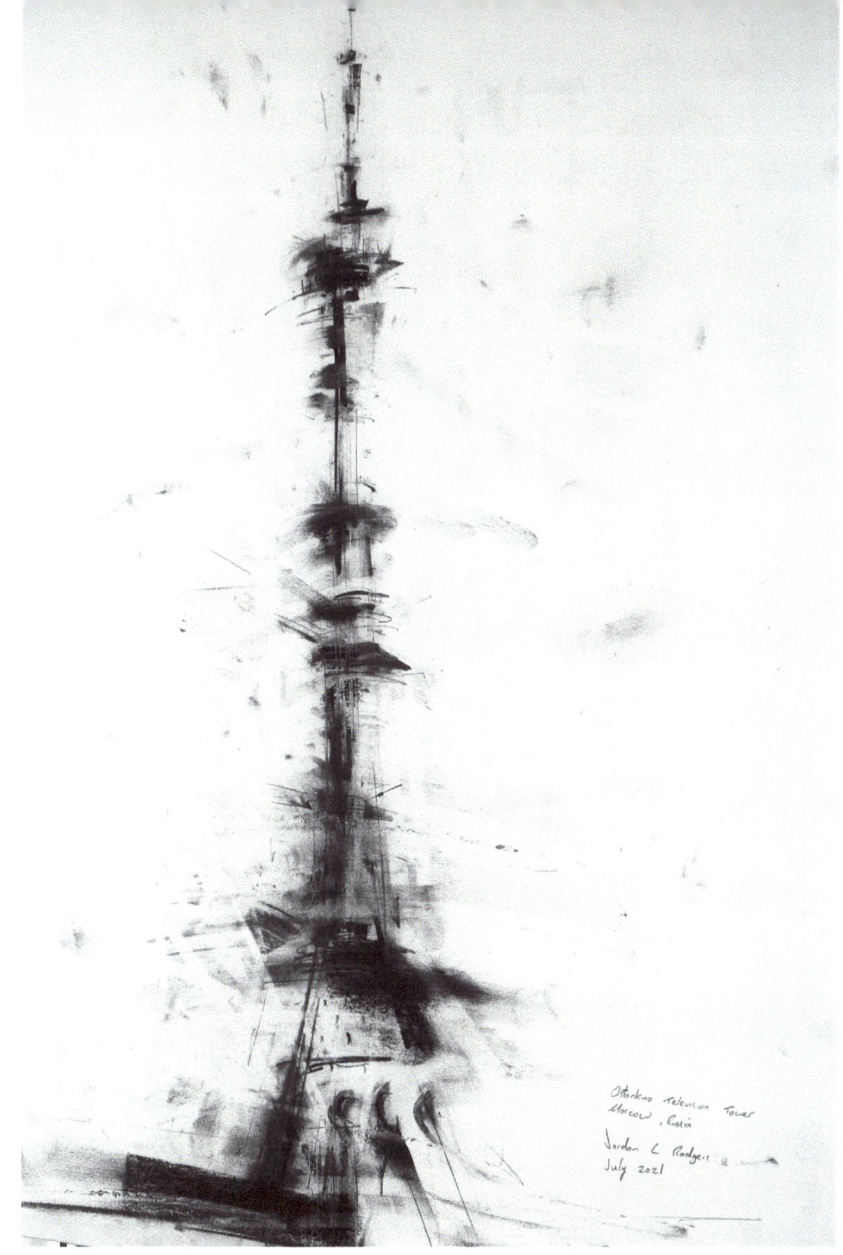

Ostankino Television Tower

Останкинская Телебашня

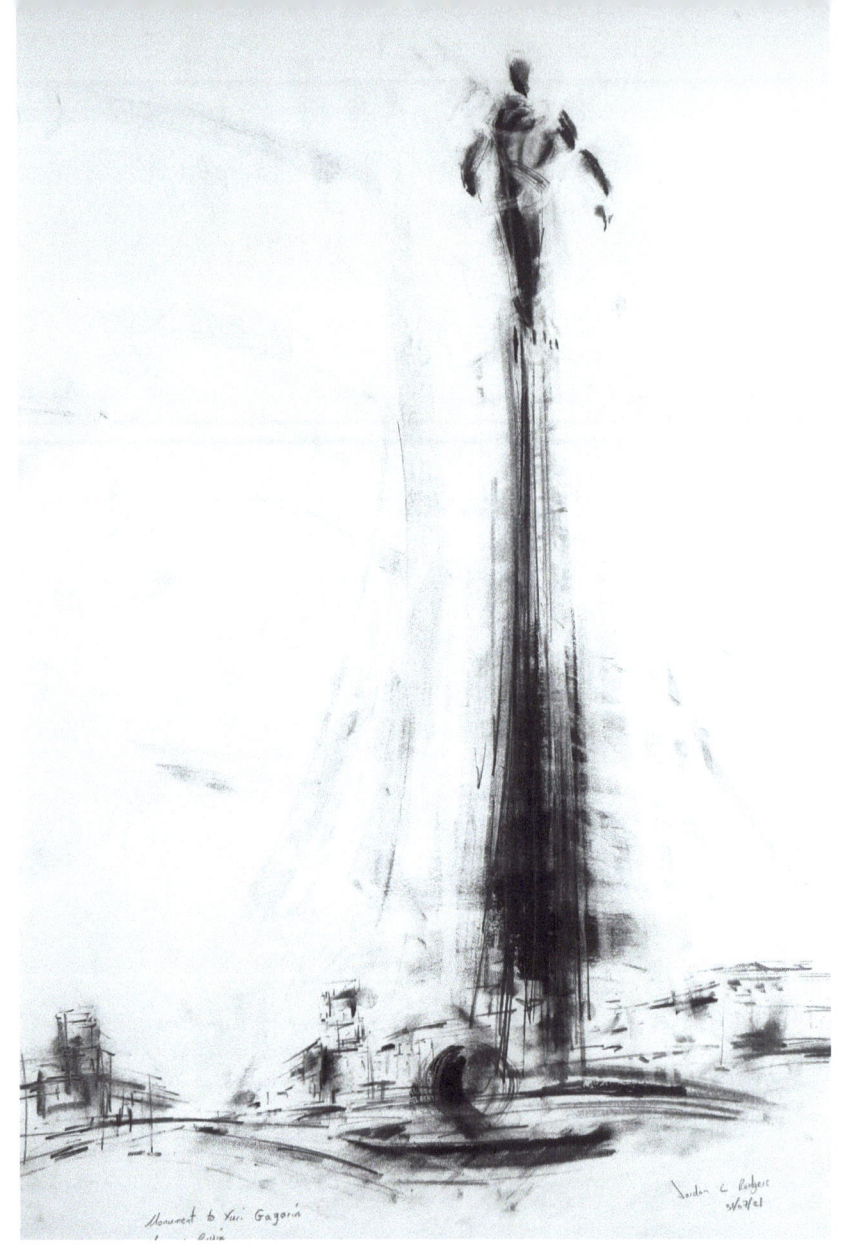

Monument to Yuri Gagarin

Памятник Ю.А. Гагарину

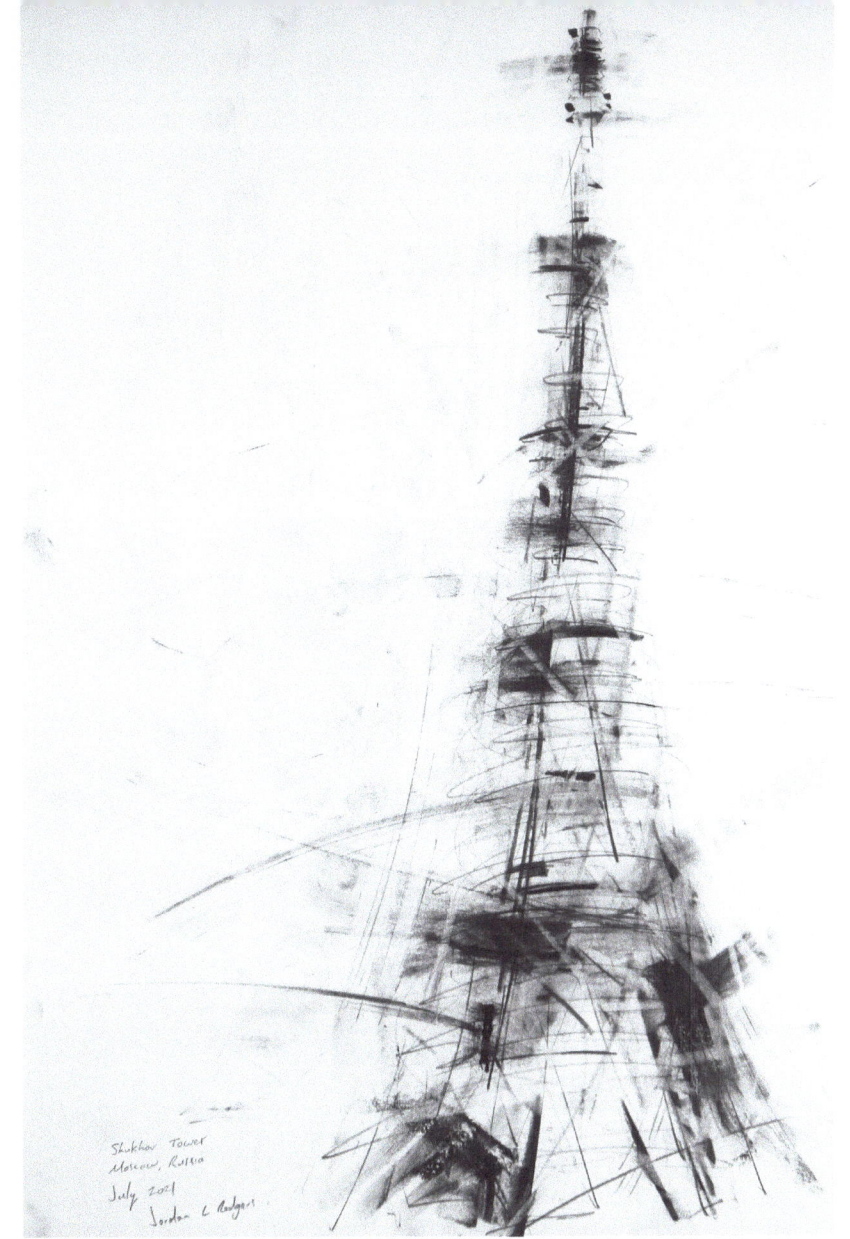

Shukhov Tower

23

Шуховская башня

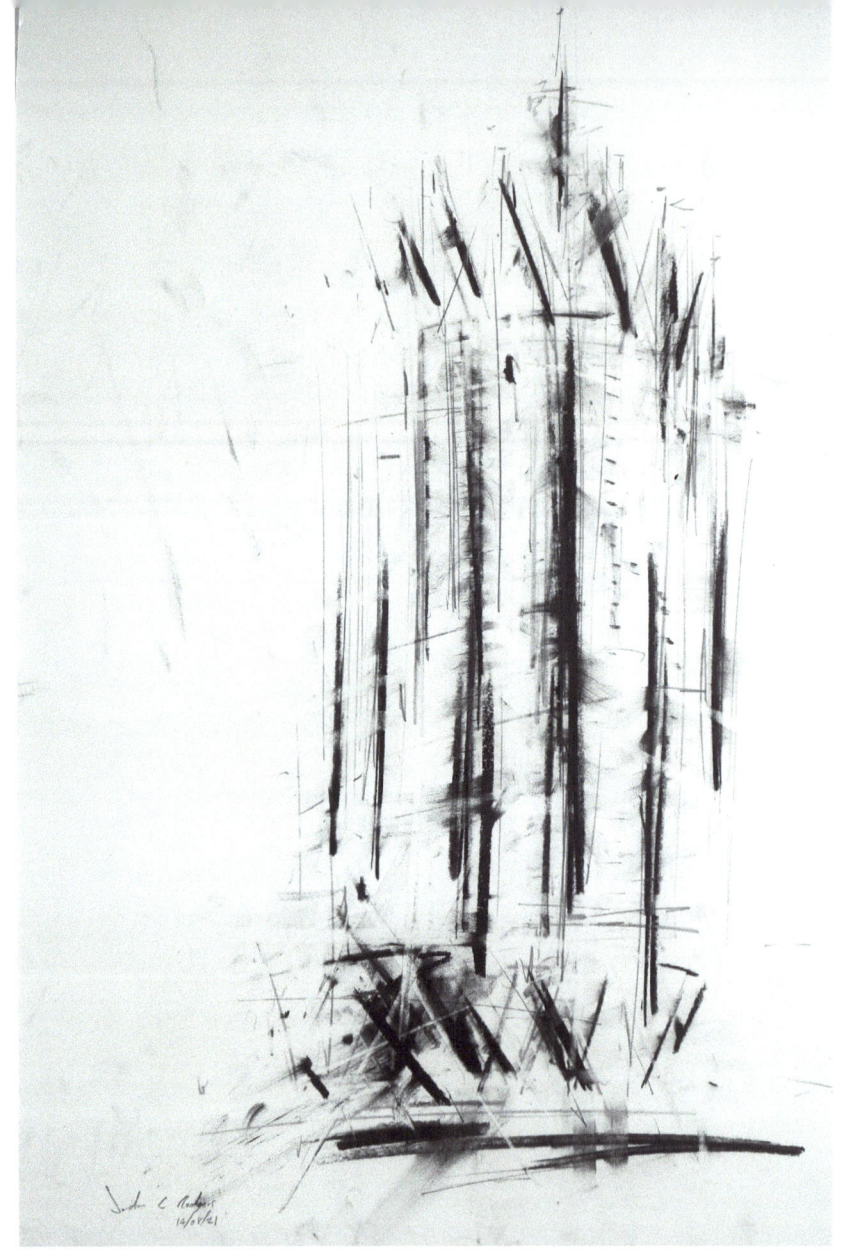

Russian State Scientific Center for Robotics and Technical Cybernetics

Цнии робототехники

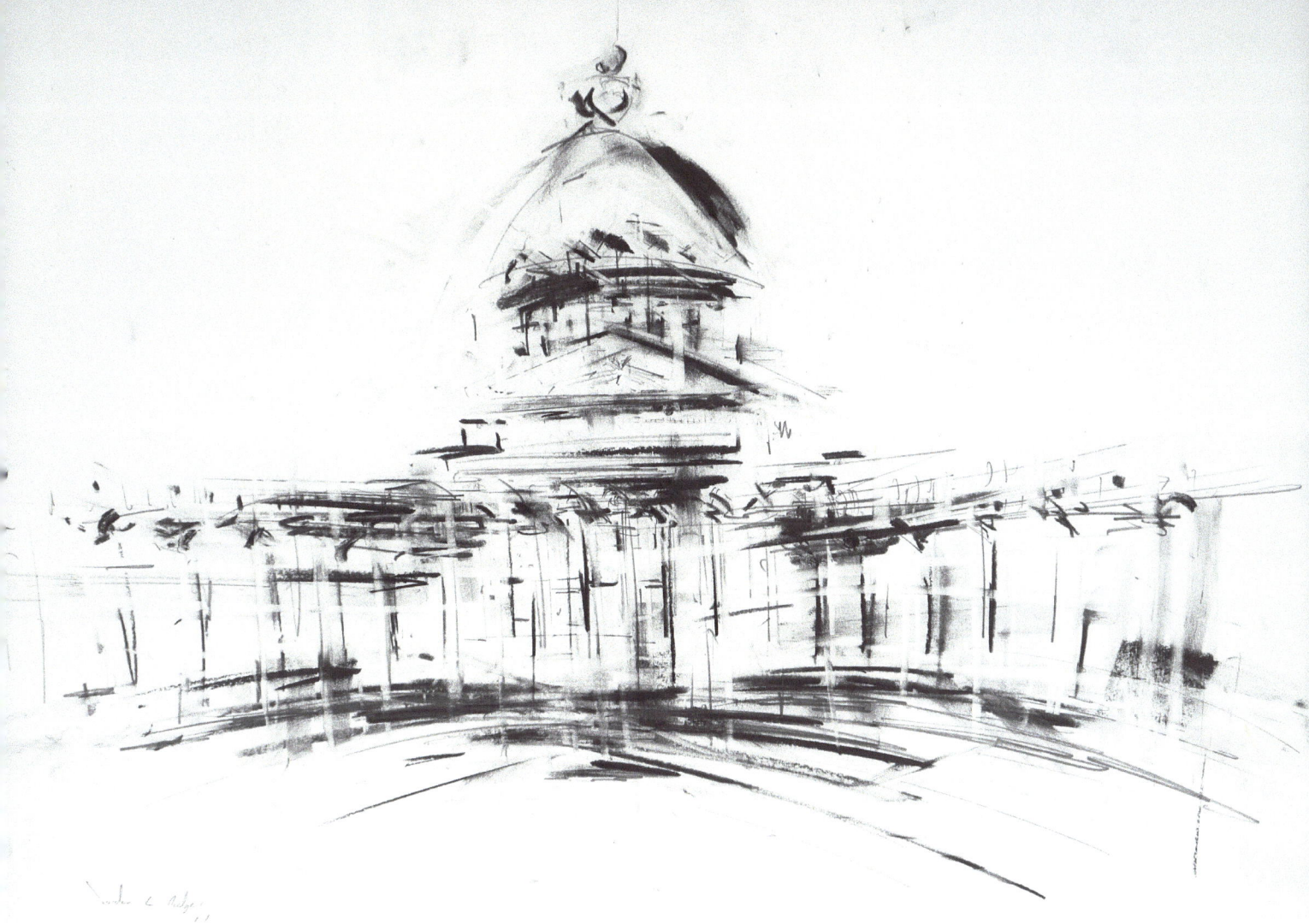

Kazan Cathedral

25

Казанский кафедральный собор

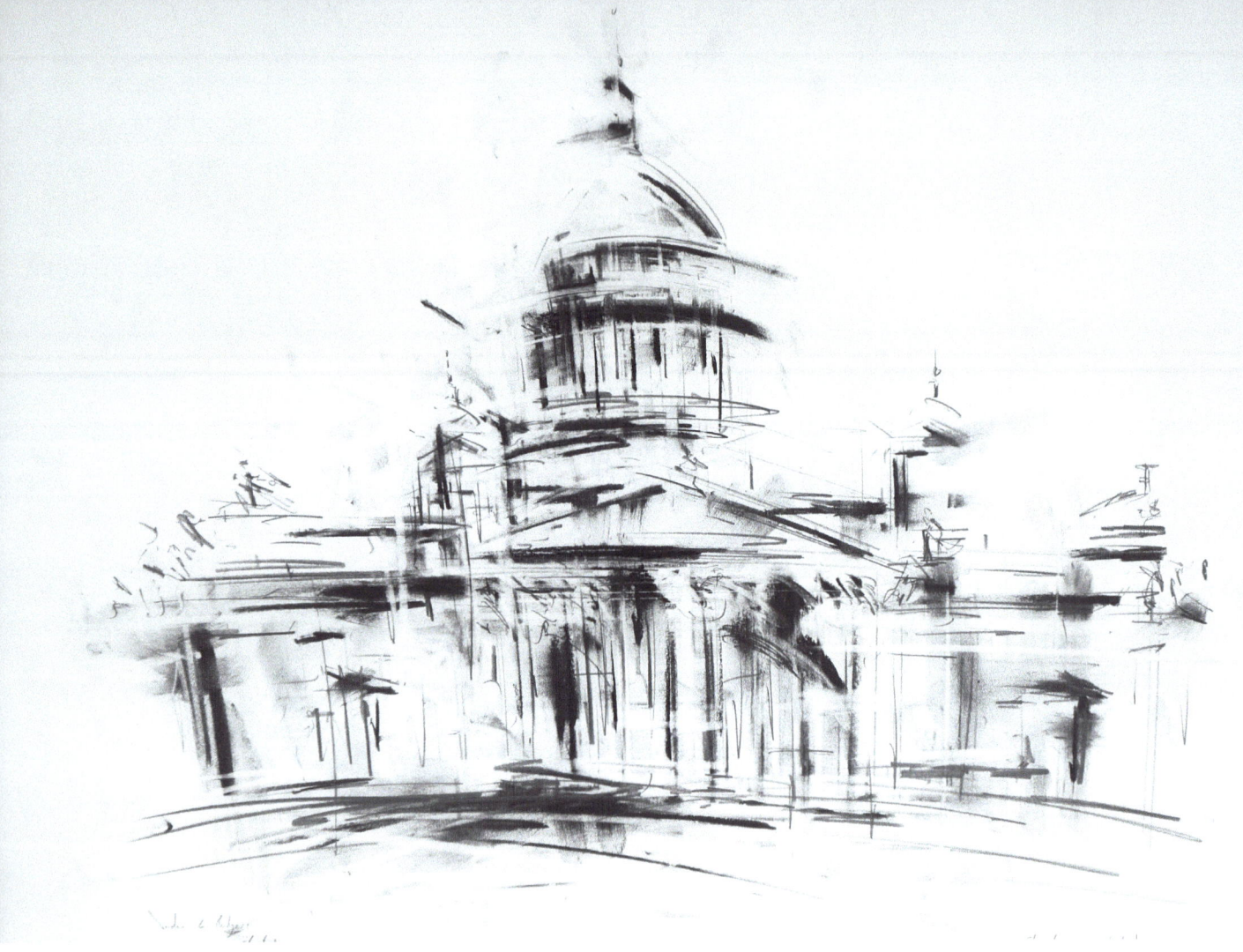

Saint Isaac's Cathedral

26

Исаа́киевский Собо́р

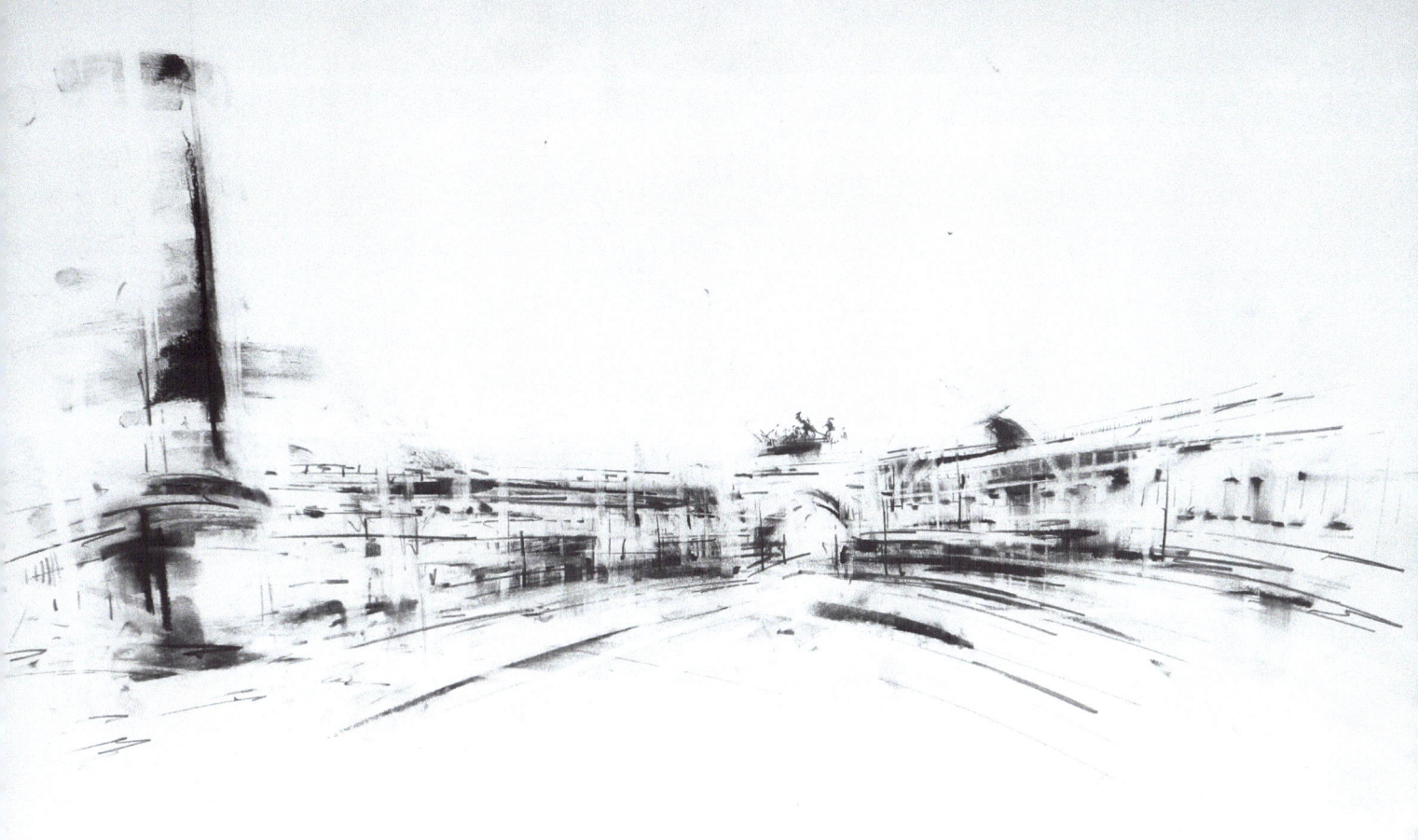

Palace Square

Дворцовая площадь

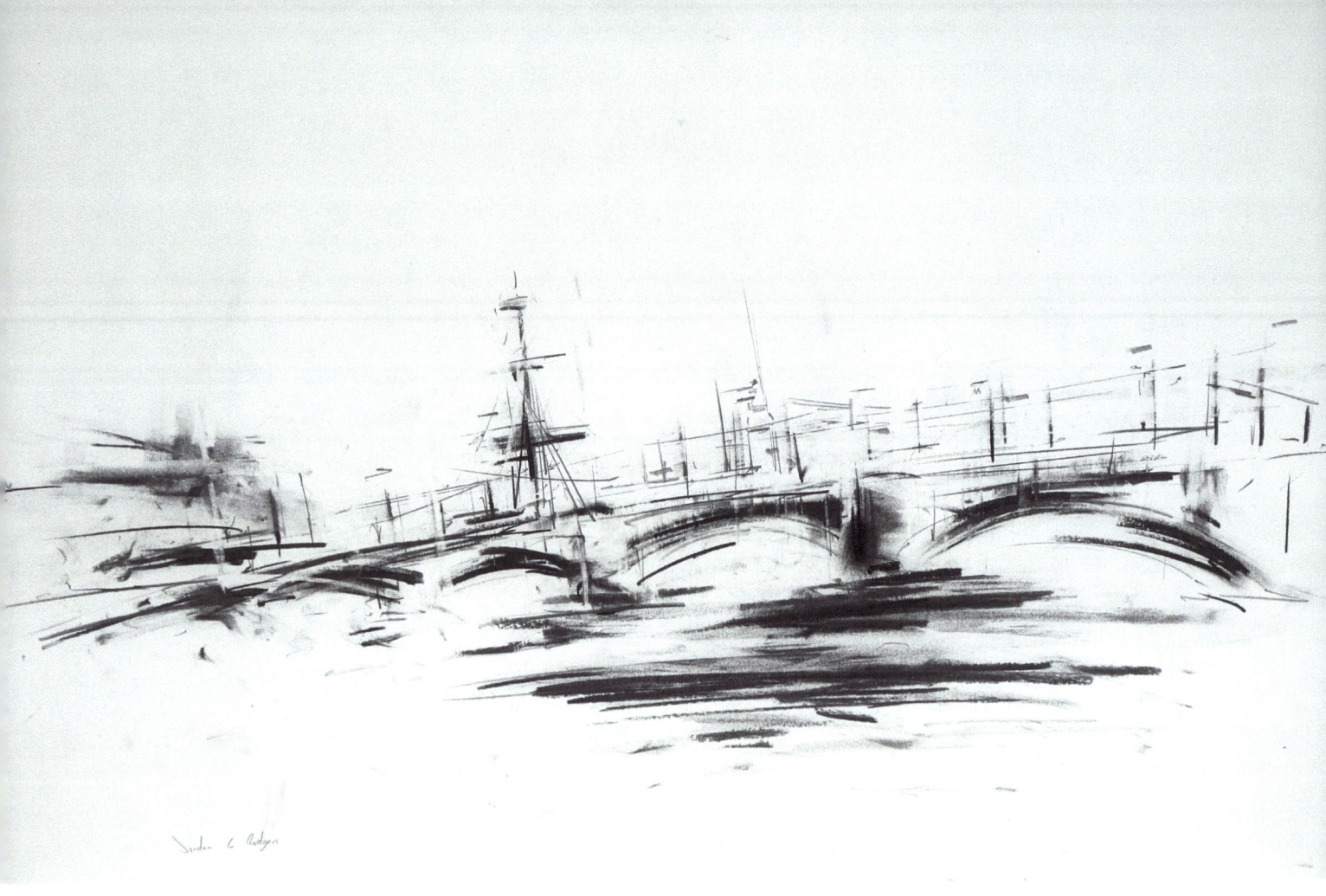

Birzhevoy bridge

28

Биржевой мост

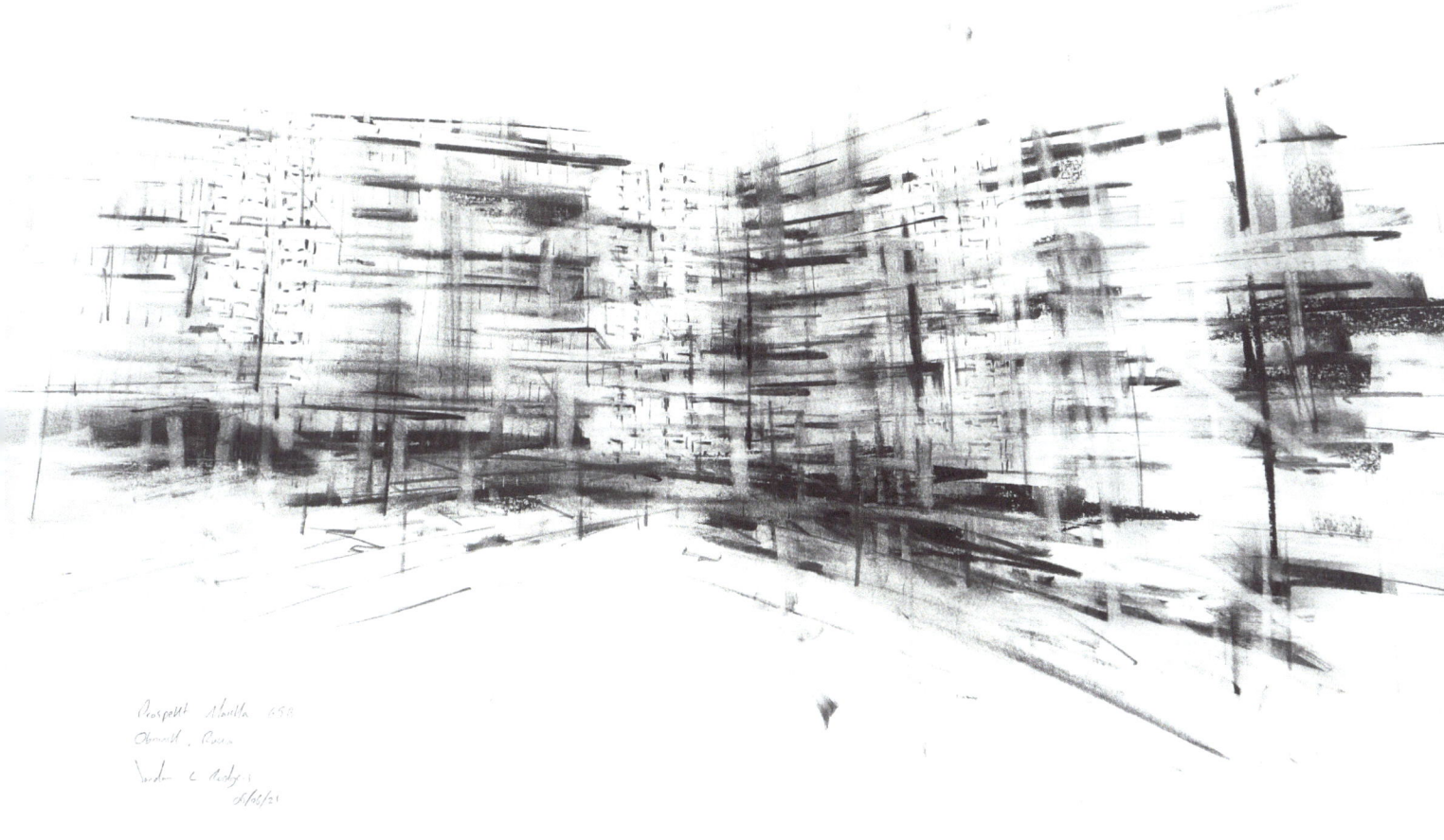

Prospekt Marksa, 65, Obninsk

Проспект Маркса, 65, Обнинске

Prospekt Marksa, 78, Obninsk

Проспект Маркса, 78, Обнинске

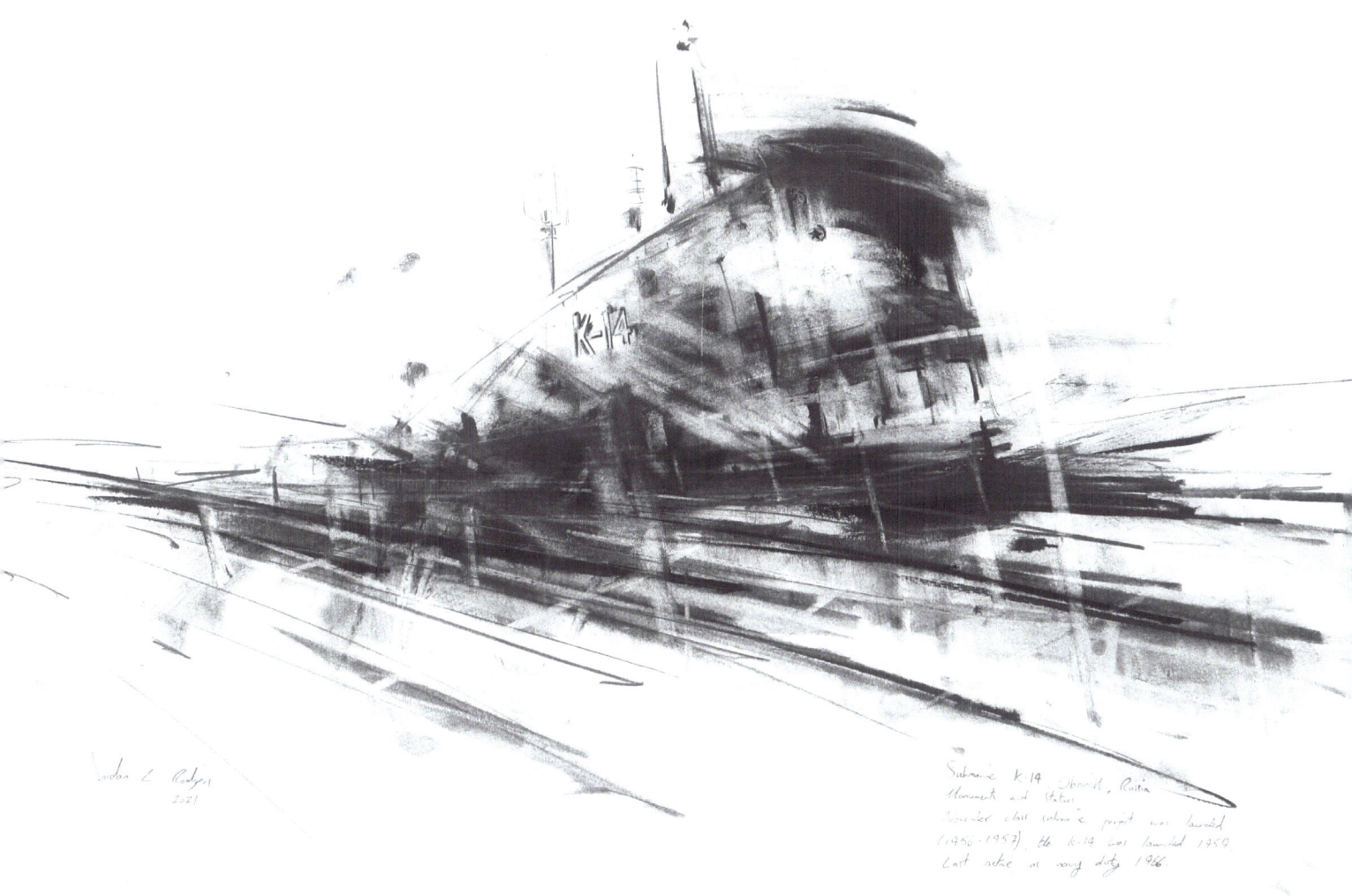

Cabin K-14 at the memorial to the First Ascents of the Submarine Nuclear Fleet in Obninsk

Рубка К-14 в мемориале «Первопроходам подводного атомного флота» в Обнинске

International Book Publications Publisher: Amazon and Blurb

Socialist Modernism Architecture Drawing: Eastern Bloc Paperback – by Jordan L Rodgers, 2021
Language: English and Polish

Socialist Modernism Architecture Drawing: Germany Paperback – by Jordan L Rodgers, 2021
Language: English and German

Socialist Modernism Architecture Drawing: Russia Paperback – by Jordan L Rodgers, 2021
Language: English and Russian

Socialist Modernism Architecture Drawing: Ukraine Paperback – by Jordan L Rodgers, 2021
Language: English and Ukrainian

Katowice Sketchbook Paperback – by Jordan L Rodgers 2021
Language: English and Polish

Russia Sketchbook 2021 (Скетчбук Россия 2021) Paperback – by Jordan L Rodgers, 2021
Language: English

Charcoal Architecture Drawing Russia (Рисунки углём архитектуры в России) Paperback – by Jordan L Rodgers, 2021
Language: English and Russian

Śląsk węglem szkicowany Paperback – by Jordan L Rodgers, 2020
Language: English and Polish

Charcoal Mining UK Paperback – by Jordan L Rodgers, 2020
Language: English

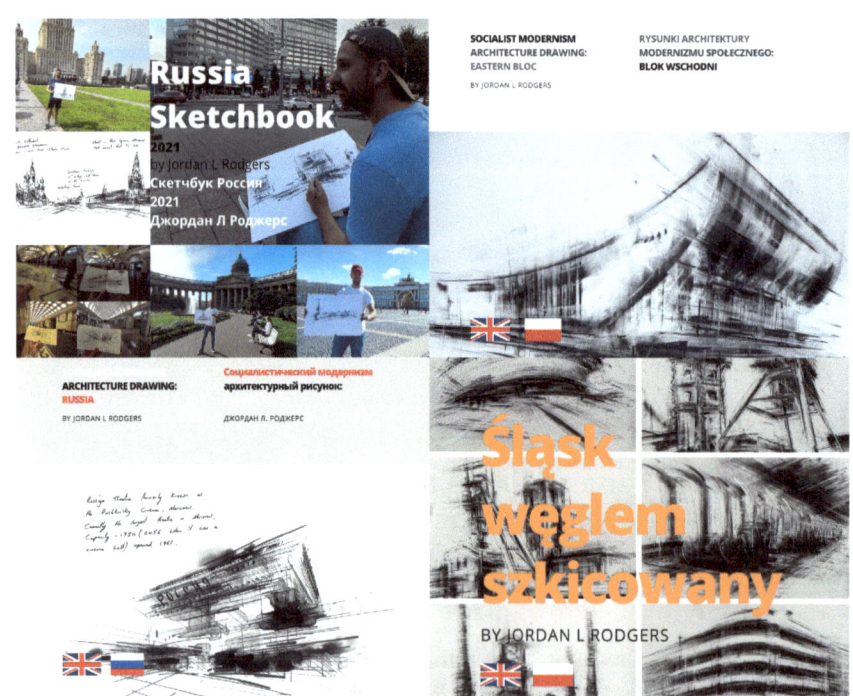

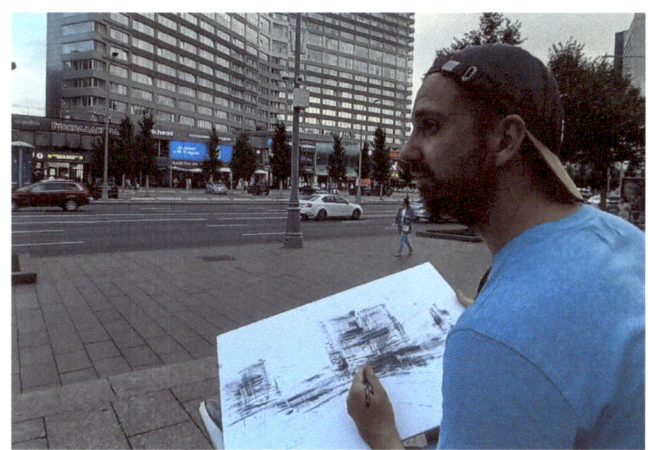
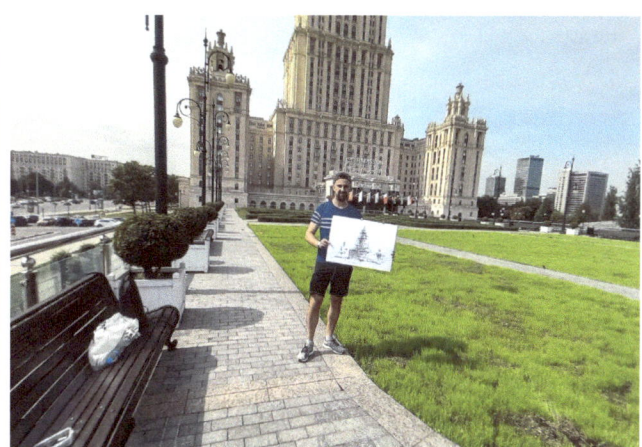
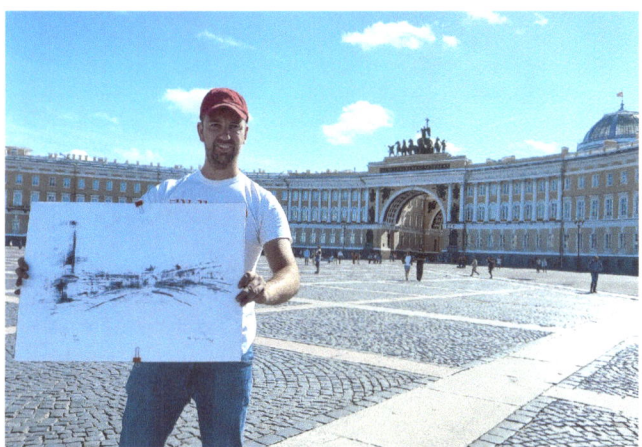
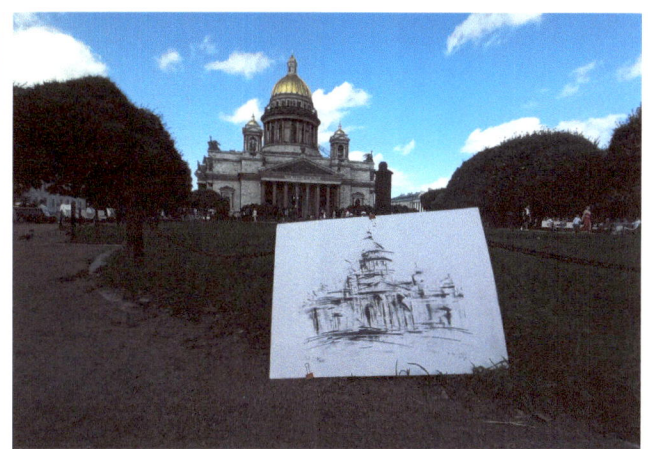
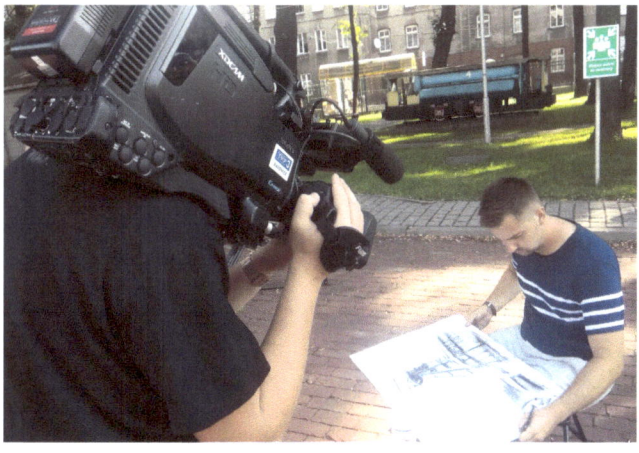
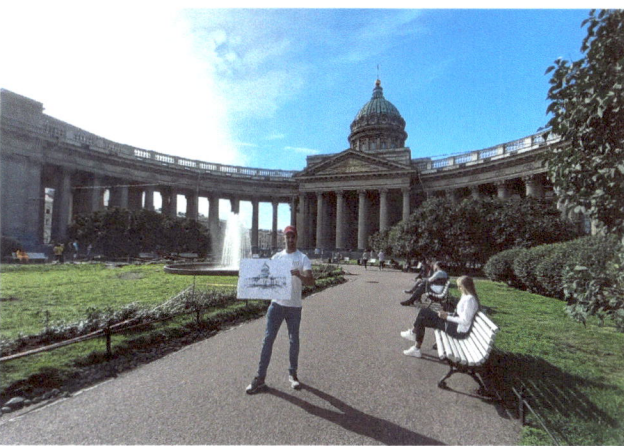

www.ingramcontent.com/pod-product-compliance
Lightning Source LLC
Chambersburg PA
CBHW051821210526
45473CB00005B/1692